Darkness Walks

Darkness Walks
The Shadow People Among Us

Jason Offutt

ANOMALIST BOOKS
*San Antonio * New York*

An Original Publication of Anomalist Books

Darkness Walks
Copyright © 2009 by Jason Offutt
ISBN: 1933665378

Cover image: Crystal Hollis

Book design by Seale Studios

For information, go to anomalistbooks.com or write to:
Anomalist Books, 5150 Broadway #108, San Antonio, TX 78209

TABLE OF CONTENTS

A big "thank you" to my wife Kimberly and my sister Jana Bunch who read this book before anyone else (and corrected many of my mistakes along the way), the faculty of Northwest Missouri State University's English and Physics departments, Ryan Straub for his diligent research, and the experts and victims of the entities discussed in Darkness Walks. *This book is dedicated to you all and to everyone who's ever experienced something they can't explain.*

FOREWORD

To my recollection Shadow People became a hot topic on the late radio night talk shows about 2002 or so. Suddenly, it seemed that no program could be deemed a success unless it had at least a few callers who spoke of their spooky experiences with these entities who were darker than the darkness. I remember appearing as a guest on *Coast to Coast* at this time and having Art Bell announce that I had been pursuing Shadow People for years, so perhaps I could explain what they were.

Well, I could not.

I responded with a definition about what the Shadow People meant in terms of some Native American tribal folklore, but I explained that the topic of Shadow People was so broad and so dramatically nuanced with individual responses to the phenomenon that a single all-purpose definition was out of the question. To deal with the Shadow People adequately would require a book.

We now have such a book in Jason Offutt's *Darkness Walks*.

Jason admits that he saw Shadow People when he was a child in the 1970s. I saw them when I was a child back in the late 1930s, early 1940s. At first they frightened me, but they appeared almost nightly to my sister and me. They never did any physical harm to us, so we learned not to fear them. When I was a child, they were just "the people who came at night." Later, I concluded that they were ghosts.

Since that time, I have come to believe that Shadow People are not just one "thing," but our name for a great variety of entities. Shadow People is a collective title for many different manifestations of the metaphysical, the mystical, the magical, and the metaphorical.

On occasion, I have thought of the Shadow People in terms of a reflection that Herman Hesse (author of

Siddhartha and *Steppenwolf*) shared in his *Autobiographical Writings:* "...I do not know when I saw him for the first time: I think he was always there, that he came into the world with me. The little man was a tiny, gray, shadowy being, a spirit or goblin, angel or demon, who at times walked in front of me in my dreams as well as during my waking hours, and whom I had to obey, more than my father, more than my mother, more than reason, yes, often more than fear."

I am quite convinced that Shadow People have always been with us. As beings from another level of our multidimensional universe, I theorize that they might at times be summoned by human emotions, especially fear and self-doubt. I also believe that very often they are invited into a human's personal psychic space by an individual's careless dabbling in the occult. Jason Offutt has a very good chapter dealing with that aspect of the mystery in "Ouija Boards and Other Invitations to Shadows."

As I have stated, the subject of Shadow People defies any single definition. Offutt's excellent study of the phenomenon presents us with the most thorough and complete work yet written regarding the mysterious beings that we have come to call collectively, the Shadow People.

In *Darkness Walks,* Offutt initially presents the night visitors as the mystery that they are, then he works his way through a wide range of manifestations. He covers a great many very eerie, shadowy twists and turns, and he does not neglect examining those arguments which question whether the beings are benign or dangerous. Jason may not have any ultimate answers, but no one has done a better job of defining who or what these shades might be.

– Brad Steiger, author of
the *Shadow World* series

INTRODUCTION

The paranormal has always fascinated me. From ghosts, UFOs and Bigfoot to Frankenstein's monster, Dracula and the Triffids, my Saturday afternoons were filled with monster movies and my nights were filled with books about flying saucers. To me there was some comfort in the grotesque, the inhuman, the unknown. Maybe it was the fact that there were some things in the universe for which science had no answer. Or maybe, even as a child I realized the more knowledge you possess, the less frightening those things that go bump in the night become ... all except one.

I knew about Shadow People long before they became buzzwords on paranormal talk radio and the internet. In the mid-1970s, Shadow People thrust themselves into my life and, although the visitations were never pleasant, they were never threatening. Decades have past, but my childhood encounters have fueled my curiosity and driven me to discover what these entities are. I make no claims that I know what Shadow People are. I approached this topic as a journalist, allowing others – experts, victims, willing participants – to tell their stories.

In doing so, I hope this book answers some of your questions about the Shadow People, and I hope you find comfort in knowing many others have witnessed these entities as well. You are not alone anymore.

Jason Offutt
Maryville, Missouri
June 29, 2008

CHAPTER ONE

The Mystery of Shadow People

Sunlight drifted through the open window of the girls' bedroom as they played dolls. Kara and Sarah were sitting on their bunk beds when they realized they weren't alone – the Shadow Man was watching them.

"We saw it only once but talked about it often throughout our childhood," Kara said. "I told my sister to go get (our dolls) that were on the floor near the door."

Sarah slowly shook her head "no" as she stared apprehensively at the door.

Kara slowly turned to see what kept her sister from moving. "I saw the dark silhouette of a man," she said. "Just the head and shoulders, leaning into the doorway from outside it as if he was peeking in."

The mid-afternoon sunlight dressing the room made no harsh shadows, especially not one shaped like a man. "It was broad daylight and the shape was opaque black and seemed to be two-dimensional, just like a shadow," Kara said. "I really don't remember what we did after that, but I do remember telling our mom about it and she just thought we were being silly. The memory is very real, and I am sure if I asked my sister about it today – 30 years later – she would describe it just as I did."

As Kara and Sarah discovered, sometimes Shadows do walk. In the gray world of our homes after the sun goes down, we sometimes glimpse the black shapes of people – or animals – moving through our bedrooms, our hallways, our waking nightmares. They walk, they stare, and sometimes … they talk. They are the Shadow People, and I've found stories about them from across North America, England, Portugal, South Africa, Australia, and other parts of our planet. Out of these stories have emerged eight general categories of Shadow People:

- Benign Shadows,
- Shadows of Terror,
- Red-Eyed Shadows,
- Noisy Shadows,
- Angry Hooded Shadows,
- Shadows that Attack,
- Shadow Cats,
- and The Hat Man.

These categories often overlap. Some terrifying Shadow People have red eyes, some don't. Some Hat Men are ominous, some are not. Some Angry Hooded Shadows seem to paralyze you and sometimes attack, others simply seem to acknowledge your presence before they make their way through your house and disappear through a wall. But what they are is a mystery. Are these Shadow People ghosts? Demons? Reflections from a parallel dimension? Space aliens? Or, as with Ebenezer Scrooge's ghosts, maybe "an undigested bit of beef, a blot of mustard, a crumb of cheese, a fragment of underdone potato."

Although experts in the paranormal – and science – offer numerous explanations for these Shadow People, all, or none, may be valid. Whatever these entities are, the uncountable number of geographically separated people who have encountered these dark beings know they are real because they have reported seeing, hearing, feeling, and fearing these walking Shadows – like Margot Davies of Seattle. Davies moved into a house just east of Seattle in 2002 and, from early on she knew something wasn't quite right about the house.

"The third night in the house, some relatives came to stay the night," she said. "Later the next morning my aunt took me aside and said she sensed something in the house the previous night."

Nothing bothered her until she began modeling in 2005 and started seeing a dark figure in her home. "Quite often I began to see a dark shape of person near the door of the den out of the corner of my eye," she said.

At first she dismissed these sightings as a trick of mind until she was sitting in her hot tub one night in November 2007. "I glanced in the living room window and there was a dark Shadow in front of the lamp staring at me," she said. "At first I thought someone was in the house, but then how could they be dark in front of a bright lamp?"

As soon as this man-shaped Shadow realized she was looking at it, it quickly moved from the window through the living room wall, remerged in the kitchen then disappeared towards the den.

"I ran inside dripping wet, checked the house and no one was inside," she said. "I never said anything to anyone."

A few months later, a cousin stayed the night with her and saw the same thing. "He looked awful in the morning," Davies said. "I asked why. He told me he was very frightened the previous night. He said he saw a Shadow in the hallway watching him in bed and then it disappeared through the wall."

Her cousin asked why she didn't warn him her house was haunted. She didn't because she didn't think it was haunted. "I'm not sure it's a ghost, and if it is, I don't think it's a bad one," Davies said. "I'm not sure what this Shadow Person is or what it wants. I don't feel threatened by it, but I am scared when I see it. Sightings are rare though, so I don't mind putting up with it as an unwelcome houseguest."

Jason Offutt

What Are They?

Have *you* seen these human figures walking through your room at night? Have they been cloaked like the Grim Reaper? Have they glared at you from the darkness with glowing, red eyes? Or, worse, have they touched you? I know you have a story, or you probably wouldn't be reading this book.

Do you know what these Shadow People are? Carl Beckham's father thought he did. Shortly after Beckham's father died in 1992, Beckham discovered something he could never wipe from his mind.

"My brother told me that one night he was bringing my dad home from the doctor's office," he said. "When they got to the house my dad told him to pull his car so that he could shine the headlights into the back yard because he wanted to see what was out there."

Beckham's brother saw nothing strange in the backyard, but since their father slept in the back of the house, his room would have overlooked the yard. Beckham wondered what his father was looking for.

"When I went into his room I was shocked to see that he had placed several homemade locks – pieces of wood nailed onto the door – like he was trying to keep something out," Beckham said.

Beckham's father saw blacker-than-night spirits roaming the yard, spirits he was afraid fed off the dying. Although no one else in the family could see these Shadow People, Beckham's father could, and he was terrified of them.

Terror often accompanies these entities; sometimes because of the unknown, but other times just the presence of a Shadow Man pulls raw fear to the surface of your consciousness. Independence, Missouri-based psychic Margie Kay is familiar with Shadow People, and said these entities come from a number of different sources, but that one type of Shadow Person feeds off terror.

"I think that Shadow People are just people that live in a higher dimension than us, and they may look just like us on the Other Side, but we can only see their outline," Kay said. "Most are probably benign, but others – the ones who actually interact with us – are likely not and may even be some other type of entity who gets their energy from fear."

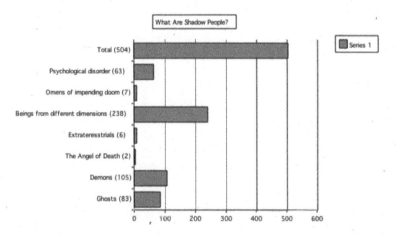

In a poll conducted on my blog (from-the-shadows.blogspot.com), respondents overwhelmingly believed Shadow People are beings from different dimensions (47%), over demons (21%), ghosts (16%), psychological disorders (13%), omens of impending doom (1%), extraterrestrials (1%) and the angel of death (0%). But evidence supports Shadow People may be all of these – and more.

A Little History

Shadow entities have been part of our cultural mythos presumably forever. But specific descriptions of Shadow People can be traced back to recent history with an 1887 short story, "Le Horla," by French author Guy de Maupassant. Details of paranormal activity in Maupassant's story correspond with many Shadow People reports. Maupassant's fictional tale, which deals with an aristocrat's descent into madness, describes a fear of sleep, seeing a dark presence in the periphery, and finally feeling the presence become more invasive to the point of attack.

The terror that Maupassant's character experiences is common in many Shadow People encounters: "Last night I felt that somebody was squatting on me, putting his mouth on mine, drinking my life out through my lips," the character says. "Yes, I really felt he was sucking my life out through my throat, just like a leech would do." Maupassant's character later postulates he is possessed by this entity that has stalked him. This, again, is a behavior reported in some Shadow People encounters.

The term "Shadow People" appeared in popular culture in 1953 in the radio drama "Creatures in the Shadows" (also known by the title "The Shadow People") that appeared on Chicago's WGN-AM "Hall of Fantasy." But the earliest Shadow People report I have been able to uncover occurred to Charles G. Parcells, now of Otto, North Carolina, in 1949.

"My encounter was a long time ago, but I still remember it very well," Parcells said. "Of course, at the time it occurred I'm sure the term Shadow Man had not yet been coined."

Charles was 13 years old and lived with his mother, brother, and grandmother in San Jose, California, when a Shadow Man invaded his life. "It was around 10 at night, with just the faint glow of street lights visible through the windows," he said. "My brother and I were lying in our beds, talking a bit before going to sleep."

Diagonally from Charles was an old-fashioned sash window – not curtained or shaded – which looked out over a walkway that ran alongside the house. "All at once, a dark figure dressed in a black cloak and wearing a black hat with a wide brim and a tall crown, appeared in the window," he recalled. "No facial features were discernible on this 'person,' but I took it to be a man."

The Shadow Man stood at the window, reached out both hands, and in complete silence raised the bottom sash. "I thought he was going to climb in," Parcells said. "At that moment I started yelling my head off in total fear. As I did so, the figure reached up and silently closed the window, turned and moved out of sight."

His mother burst into the room to see what the yelling was about. "I need not go into that scene," Parcells said, "since my tale was profoundly doubted." But the next day, Charles discovered that the Shadow Man was something more than a flesh-and-blood man.

"The window had been locked from the inside the whole time," he said. "The window, either opening or closing, made an audible raspy, squeaky sound." Outside no footprints dotted the soft earth between the window and the walkway. "But I saw something, so what in the hell was it?"

This book contains hundreds of such first-hand accounts of these Shadow People. Many of the people whose stories appear in this book requested anonymity, and those people I only refer to by first name. As a journalist, I collected stories from face-to-face interviews, telephone interviews, email, and comments posted on my blogs (From-the-Shadows.blogspot.com and Shadowpeoplebook.blogspot.com).

But this book isn't just a collection of Shadow People stories; it's an attempt to explain this phenomenon from the viewpoints of physics, psychology, metaphysics, Western religion, and American Indian shamanism. Many people believe Shadow People are beings from different dimensions. Others think these walking Shadows are demons, ghosts, a psychological disorder, extraterrestrials, the Angel of Death, or omens of impending doom. This book also covers how to get rid of the Shadow. I wish I'd had this book when I was a child, watching in horror as these entities walked in fits and jerks through my room.

My quest to find out more about these darker-than-night, two-dimensional, human-shaped beings started many years ago. Between the ages of 8 and 12 years, I saw this walking darkness. Lying in bed at night, after my parents turned off the lights, moonlight pouring through the open windows in our old farm house gave me a clear view of my entire room – the bookshelf, the Farrah Fawcett poster, and the Shadow People. I stared from behind blankets as human shadows walked through my room. I'd cry out, and Mom and Dad rushed to my room, but they never saw the things I saw. I didn't know what the things were, but I knew I saw them. As I grew older, I found more people have seen these Shadow People, and have been just as frightened.

Whatever the explanation – or explanations – for these Shadow Beings, most people who encounter them feel afraid, violated, and helpless. "To a Shadow Person you are nothing, and that's why they will sometimes ignore someone," exorcist James Bucknam said. "If you strike their curiosity, then look out, their presence means bad things are on the way." Shadow People, he said, never operate alone and are very curious. "They investigate everything, and are constantly checking people out," he said. "Be careful with Shadow People. They attract other negative entities as well that are floating around out there looking for something to attach to." Bucknam is convinced Shadow People have never been human, and exist in negative realms – always looking for a way into our world. "Shadow People are part of the world of spirit," he said. "And they are bad news."

Gary G. Ford of Calgary, Alberta, Canada, has seen them, too, and challenges those who don't acknowledge Shadow People. "They are enough to scare the works out of most people who want to deny these experiences can happen," Ford said. "But I've experienced them. I know they are real, and that makes the universe more complicated than simple-minded theoreticians wish to entertain."

So begins our journey through a land where Shadows lurk, Shadows walk, and Shadows dance – and we're just in the way.

CHAPTER 2

The Science of Shadow People

Science rules the universe. If you drop a hammer, it falls. If you drop a hammer and a tennis ball, they fall at the same rate. If you see something that isn't physically there, it may be something biochemical or electrical dancing on your brain. But how do these rules apply in the paranormal universe? In this chapter, I will look into physics, psychology, and neuroscience in an attempt to deconstruct the Shadow People, those creatures that appear to be both solid and vapor, a waking nightmare and a sleep disorder, a real entity looming over you and the product of electric stimulation to the brain.

Basic Physics

Margie Kay of Independence, Missouri, relates a story told by her 11-year-old granddaughter Cynthia about an encounter with a Shadow Person. "She said that one night she woke up in the middle of the night to see an outline of a six-foot-tall person standing in her room, looking away from her at the TV set that had come on apparently by itself," Margie said. "The person turned around and looked at her for a few seconds, then just dissolved away. She said it had no features. She did not sleep the rest of the night and wouldn't even get out of bed to turn off the TV until it was daylight."

To Northwest Missouri State University (NWMSU) chemistry and physics professor Rick Toomey, something solid enough to cast a shadow – and hold its shape – can't just dissolve. Matter comes in three forms: gas, liquid and solid, and only gas dissipates into the air. "If it's not solid or liquid it has to be vapor. Gasses don't maintain shape," he said. "And you'd need a pretty high density of gas to prevent the transmission of light."

So for Shadow People to exist according to physics, Toomey said, they have to be pretty dense. "It has to be a physical entity that's solid. It's not liquid. It's not gas," Toomey said. "That's why I have a problem with ghosts opening doors. A gas isn't going to surround a doorknob and apply torque. I can't buy into it."

Toomey's colleague in the NWMSU physics department, Dave Richardson, shares Toomey's concern. Given the many reports of Shadow People walking through someone's bedroom, they have to be solid. "If you just look at what a shadow actually means, when they're produced there must be a blockage of light somehow, or the removal of light in some way," he said. "From a scientist's point of view they have to be opaque. Unless it was incredibly dense, the gas wouldn't do much." For example, smoke casts a shadow, but can't retain a shape and quickly dissipates. For Cynthia's shadow to look like a man and to turn on the television, it has to be something else. "It seems a difficult thing to actually reconcile with what we know about light and shadows," Richardson said.

But what of Shadow People who can exert a physical force? Like the experience of Donny from Montana: "I was sleeping on my side when I was awoken by what felt like someone sitting on my bed behind me," he said. "I felt someone sticking their finger to the middle of my back." When he opened his eyes, three Shadow Beings stood around his bed, and he was afraid to look at what might be poking him from behind. Donny had felt a touch, although the entities slowly dissipated.

Those two events don't correspond to known science. "Physically we can't feel the force extended by gas particles," Toomey said. "In order for you to feel pressure, you have to scuba dive or somebody drops a rock on your head. You have to have a mass to exert a physical force."

So for Donny to have felt someone sitting on his bed, and a poke in the back, something solid had to be in his room. "To have a physical push, you have to have matter," Toomey said. "What matter do you have? Solid, liquid, gas. From that point you don't have many places to go. If you're feeling a touch, there has to be a push as far as physics is concerned."

Of course, many believe Shadow People aren't science. "People say 'it's not a physical force, it's an ethereal force,'" Toomey said. "Gravity only works in one direction. How many times did light knock you down?"

But people don't have to be touched to feel, as Riaan, of Cape Town, South Africa, discovered when he reached into a Shadow Person. "I was lying in bed getting ready to slumber off, when I noticed that in the corner where my bed was placed there seemed to be a exceptionally dark and dense patch," Riaan said. "I told myself that it's nothing but a play of light, shadows created by my curtains."

As Riaan laid there, his imagination running scenarios through his mind – is it a light trick? An intruder? A ghost? – he extended his arm and reached into the void. "I stuck out my hand and slowly moved it so that I can touch the corner of the wall, which was not very visible due to this 'dark patch,'" he said. "As my hand 'touched' this 'patch' I got a sudden sensation that can be equaled to having a little shock, similar to static electricity."

Riaan snapped his arm away from the dark patch. His arm "suddenly started to feel very lame with needles and pins crawling all over my skin," he said. "It felt like my skin was contracting and getting very tight and I lost all mobility in my arm."

Although Richardson agrees that something has to be solid to physically touch something else, people can occasionally feel they're being touched without really being touched. "Maybe there was some electrical interaction," he said. "There needs to be something that raises the hair on your arm that would give you the feeling that you're being touched, like static electricity on a hairbrush." Of course, if it's an electrical field that's causing this sensation, you have more immediate problems to deal with than Shadow People. "If you're in a high enough field like that, you don't really have to be that close to it to actually feel it," Richardson said. "If you get too close, you get shocks that do hurt."

Different Dimensions

One common explanation many people give for Shadow People is that they're beings from a different dimension that somehow bleed into ours. Such is the conclusion of a paranormal investigator from California who goes by the online name Froggy. Froggy has seen Shadow People during investigations and in his personal life.

"It's interesting so many people having the same or very similar experiences," he said. "I too have had this phenomenon of being paralyzed, as if something was on top of me. My brothers have also had the 'attack,' and one brother witnessed a Shadow Person way back in the 1980s, before Shadow People was a buzz word."

During a November 2007 trip to the La Purisima Mission, Froggy photographed one. "I believe we live among many different dimensions," Froggy said. "Ghosts live in one dimension, Shadow People in another, and our dimensions can cross making it possible for us to come in contact with each other."

But how does Froggy's belief match up with science?

Marie Jones, author of *PSIence: How New Discoveries in Quantum Physics and New Science May Explain the Existence of Paranormal Phenomena*, agrees other dimensions could be a possible source for Shadow People. "In my research into quantum and theoretical physics, I came across three concepts that really opened up the possibilities to me that entities from somewhere else could be coming here, showing up as either imprinted projections, or actual semi-physical manifestations, such as poltergeists, etc.," Jones said.

One of the three concepts is parallel universes. "Theoretically, if these infinite other universes exist, we really should not physically be able to access them based upon our known laws of physics," Jones said. "Yet even theoretical physicists...entertain the thought that perhaps the laws of physics on the other side allow for some cross-over."

Jones' second concept has to do with spatial and temporal alternate dimensions. "We are told that these dimensions could be infinite in size and exist at the tip of our very noses," she said. "Again, our laws of physics do not allow us to cross into them at will... but if there is some sort of resonant synchronization of energy, perhaps a doorway is opened just long enough to allow something to slip on through."

The third possibility, Jones said, is the Zero Point Field, which is an electromagnetic energy field that fills a vacuum. "Within this field lies the landscape of time, past, present and future," she said. "Linear time is only a human illusion ... but in the quantum world there is no linear nature – it all happens at once." In this field, Jones explains, is everyone who has died, is living now and will live. "That opens the door to the possibility that certain people tap into this field for information such as remote viewing, psychic abilities, and even healing others," she said. "It also presents the possibility that entities may be coming from the field, manifesting in our level of reality, which is really just one among many levels, than vanishing back into the field." This, Jones said, could explain the nature of most ghosts and Shadow People.

Although some physicists entertain the idea of these multiple or parallel universes, Richardson and Toomey aren't among them. Said Richardson: "If [Shadow People] are solid and we kind of ignore the people who say they put their hands through them – I always hate to bring this up in this context – but if there were extra dimensions, there could be the effect of something similar. [Shadow People] might actually be people. I'm skeptical of that, but it's possible. We're just starting to figure out that sort of stuff."

Toomey's not as forgiving of the theory that makes 11 dimensions possible – String Theory, in which there are more than four dimensions, each small and stringlike. "String Theory is math, it's not science," Toomey said. "You can postulate there are 11 dimensions, you can't test it. Until String Theory produces a testable hypothesis, it's not science. It might as well be the paranormal. Inter-dimensional is about as science fiction as it gets."

Sleep Paralysis

Sardonic Laconic (an online name; he is sardonic, after all) saw the Shadow Man as a child. "The memories have haunted me ever since," he said. "When I was six, I saw it ... at my dad's new house, towering over my bed," he said. "I couldn't move, and I don't remember what happened next. All I remember is trying to scream, but there was this horrible weight on my chest."

This type of encounter is all too common, and psychology has a name for it – sleep paralysis. As an anonymous poster to my paranormal blog put it, "It's a simple physiological phenomenon, similar to sleepwalking. When you go to sleep and dream, your brain shuts down the connection to your body, so that you don't walk and thrash about in your sleep, just 'cause you're moving in your dreams. When this connection fails to shut off, you get sleepwalking. When you wake up before it can reconnect, you're paralyzed until it turns back on. End of story. No aliens, no Shadow People, just science."

April Haberyan, a psychology professor at Northwest Missouri State University, agrees that Shadow People encounters are probably the product of dreams. Haberyan said that when people sleep and enter the REM phase, "it's very common for them to see things."

Online poster Midnight Haze reported an experience somewhat similar to Sardonic Laconic's, although during the encounter, Midnight Haze was an adult. "I had lived in a two-bedroom apartment for at least twelve years," he said. "I was sleeping on my side when I was awakened by what felt like someone sitting on my bed behind me. I felt what felt like someone sticking their finger to the middle of my back and I was now paralyzed. I could not move but I could open my eyes." When he opened his eyes, there were three black figures in the corner of the room. "Two were as tall as adults and one was shorter," he said. "Now in both fear of someone behind me and the figures in the corner, I started to pray to God to help me as I closed my eyes. I opened my eyes again and the Shadows were gone and I could move again."

According to Haberyan, this kind of encounter – the fear, the paralysis, the entities – is normal. "There are hormones in REM sleep that paralyze the major muscle groups and it's called paradoxical sleep," she said. "[Although] this happens during REM, these people don't stay asleep and the hormones are still in their bodies. It can last up to eight minutes and they feel pressure on their chest and can see people – even people they know."

According to psychologists, sleep paralysis, which is known as "Old Hag Syndrome" in paranormal circles for feeling someone sitting on your chest, is relatively common. Although Carrie Moller didn't feel the pressure on her chest when she experienced Shadow People, she did, as Haberyan said, see people. "Last week [mid-June 2008], I settled myself into bed and began to drift off to sleep," Moller said. "I was dreaming while in that half-asleep stage… In this dream I was actually settled in the exact place I was settled – asleep in my bed, on my stomach, lying on the right side of my face – so in a way one could argue that I wasn't completely asleep." Then she felt something in the room, or someone. "I remember feeling the presence of people at the bottom of my bed, so – in my dream – I turned my head around and saw three or four Shadow entities shaped like people at the bottom of my bed."

Fear gripped the sleeping Moller because this dream was lucid – she knew it was real. "It seemed like they had been waiting for me to fall asleep," she said. "So I called for someone to watch over me while this was happening." She felt her body rising out of the bed and floating toward these Shadow beings. "I had no control over my actions," she said. "As I was floating towards them, they put out their arms in front of me and I immediately was pushed out back into my bed where I woke up and could remember everything vividly."

Was Carrie's encounter a dream, or was she visited by Shadow entities waiting for her to fall to sleep?

Archetypes

The black hooded figure has haunted humans for centuries. It may appear as a Shadow lurking at the periphery of vision, or it may fully reveal itself, as it did to Luke. "I've been visited by what I presume to be the same Shadow three times in my life, and the memories have haunted me ever since," he said. "I first saw it when I was two, in my bedroom at my dad's duplex."

Luke watched the hooded figure walk up the stairs and stand in his doorway before it backed away and disappeared. "When I was six, I saw it again at my dad's new house, this time towering over my bed," he said. "I couldn't move, and I don't remember what happened next. All I remember is trying to scream, but there was this horrible weight on my chest. About two years later, it poked its head into my room at my mom's house and stared at me for a moment before stepping back into the hall and disappearing." Although Luke has experienced other Shadows, the Hooded Shadow Man is the only one that frightens him. "It has always seemed very menacing," he said. "It's quite different from other Shadow People I've seen."

Reports of Shadow People are worldwide. Why would people from the United States, Europe, South Africa, and Australia see the same entity? Marie Jones is convinced it's societal. "I have spoken with many folks in the paranormal community, and many have a growing belief that these entities are a sort of archetypal presentation of the collective belief system of the times," she said. "In other words, as a collective species, we share many beliefs and paradigms, and those often manifest in our 'mythology' or how we perceive the unknown around us."

Throughout the decades, what's reported in paranormal events seems to evolve over time. For instance, with regard to UFOs, it started in the late 1800s as slow-moving airships, advancing to foo fighters buzzing planes during WWII, saucers in the 1950s, and finally today's black triangles – each incarnation keeping one step ahead of our own technology. "So, could these Shadow People in some way be [the latest] collective manifestation of our archetypal fears?" Jones asked. "We are living in tense times."

Wayne A. Chandler, associate professor of English at Northwest Missouri State University, said these ominous dark figures have had centuries to become familiar. "The features, even down to the robe the Grim Reaper wears goes back a long, long time," he said. "The idea of the Grim Reaper, the cloak and the big scythe, goes back in Europe to the Middle Ages. It's an agricultural kind of symbol; the scythe is for cutting wheat in the fall. Obviously when you cut wheat down you kill it."

Spectral figures and other aspects of the supernatural abound in classic literature, but the depiction of the paranormal in literature is quite unlike modern stories where the supernatural entity is the centerpiece of action. "In classic literature, the supernatural doesn't take action, but prompts people to take action to mess up their lives," Chandler said. "In Hamlet, there's the ghost of Hamlet's father who spurs him on to do horrible shit." And Chandler doesn't limit a culture's literature to the written word. Movies often depict the classic Grim Reaper figure (*Monty Python's The Meaning of Life*, for example), as do television programs, such as the cartoon, *The Grim Adventures of Billy and Mandy*. "I would give it a really broad definition," he said. "[Look at] movies, TV, any messages sent from the culture and you've got this figure all over the place. Art, literature, even in places the figure is not supposed to be death. In *The Lord of the Rings*, the black riders just had a sword instead of a scythe."

Tricking the Brain

Some scientific research suggests that Shadow People could be the product of electrical stimulation. While studying the effect of electric currents on the brain, Swiss neurologist Olaf Blanke obtained some unexpected results. Low-level electric currents aimed at specific regions caused a test subject – a 22-year-old college student – to physically sense a Shadow Person behind her, according to the Sept. 21, 2006, issue of *Nature*. The student kept turning her head to the right and, when asked what she was doing, she said a Shadow Person was not only standing behind her, she knew it wanted to do her harm. When the current was killed, the Shadow Person was gone. When the current was turned on again, the Shadow Person was back. Eventually, the woman reported the Shadow Person was sitting behind her trying to take things out of her hand. The fact that the actions of the Shadow Person mirrored the subject's own, led researchers to postulate that the woman's Shadow Person may be due to the electric charge, which was causing the subject to misinterpret her own actions.

A trick of light and shadow may also be to blame for many Shadow People. A team from University College London found dim lighting causes many people to see ghosts – when the context is unfamiliar. If we know what a room looks like in the daylight, we'll be less likely to mistake a coat rack for a moving, sentient entity. The less familiar we are with our surroundings, the more we'll imagine we see spooks. The researchers related this to seeing faces in clouds and carpets.

Chemist Rick Toomey said anything that throws off the chemical balance of the brain can cause all sorts of problems. "All sensation is in the nervous system and it's all chemistry," he said. "If every neurotransmitter is chemistry, you can wreak havoc with that."

Sleep paralysis, biochemical imbalances, and inter-dimensional travel are a few of the explanations proffered for some Shadow People encounters. But other encounters, dark and sinister, may have a more terrifying explanation – demons.

CHAPTER 3

The Metaphysics of Shadow People

Metaphysics represents a philosophy that digs beyond the physical world. In the Greek philosopher Aristotle's work, *Metaphysics*, he explored the nature of existence, what sort of things exist, how things can exist when the natural world is constantly changing, and the possibility/ impossibility of humans understanding existence. Today, the field of metaphysics deals with exploring that which is not seen, nor recognized by traditional science – namely, phenomena that deal with the mind. Ghosts, ESP and lucid dreaming fall into this realm, thus metaphysical explanations for Shadow People differ widely (even bringing extraterrestrials into the mix, as you'll find in Chapter 14).

Sally Rhine Feather, the Director of Development at the Rhine Research Center near the Duke University Hospital in Durham, North Carolina, said there is no metaphysical consensus when it comes to Shadow People. "I don't know if there is any one professional perspective," she said. "Some phenomena like poltergeists have been thought to be spontaneous PK (psychokinetic energy) unconsciously produced by repressed young people and possibly some haunting phenomena might even be the same thing."

Mud Shadows

In *The Active Side of Infinity*, anthropologist and author Carlos Castaneda (1925-1998) called these Shadow entities Mud Shadows. Castaneda, who catalogued paranormal discussions with his mentor Don Juan, often saw these Shadows gathering and dancing at the edge of his vision. Metaphysical author Jack Allis is an expert on Castaneda's writings and said the fear people in the presence of Shadow People feel is real – and serves a foul purpose. "These (Mud Shadows) basically feed upon human energy," Allis said.

According to Castaneda, there are two types of other-dimensional Mud Shadows – the organic entities and the inorganic entities. "The difference between the organic and the inorganic entities is the inorganic entities were just sort of shapes that could both be up to good and up to no good," Allis said. Good meaning these entities may barter for your energy; bad meaning they were out to steal it. "Some of them were up to seducing whoever they were close to. There were also the more benevolent [organic] ones." These "organic" benevolent Shadows do not feed off humans, but won't attempt to stop the "inorganic" Shadows from doing so due to a noninterference morality.

Most of Castaneda's contact with these Mud Shadows came during lucid dreaming, a dream state in which participants know they are dreaming and can, in some way, control the dream. Many people in the paranormal field equate this type of dream with astral travel. "It wasn't dreaming, as in the ordinary way we dream," Allis said. "It was actually an inter-dimensional journey," which left Castaneda – and anyone in this state – vulnerable to attack by the inorganic entities. "Some of it is very nasty," Allis said. "They were trying to capture him. What these entities are after is our energy. Their motive is to steal our energy."

Gabe, from California, has read Castaneda's work and found these Mud Shadows inserting themselves into his life. "These Shadows," he said, "are our predators. They feed off of our energy and this is why they are often seen hovering over us." As a child in Missouri, he woke to see a woman in a flowing gown hovering over his bed. "When I blinked my eyes, the woman disappeared," he said. Gabe's awareness of the figure frightened her off, but he knew why she was there – she was there to feed.

Spiritual Shadows

Psychologist Stan Gooch of England, author of *Personality and Evolution: The Biology of the Divided Self*, *The Neanderthal Legacy: Reawakening Our Genetic and Cultural Origins*, and *Creatures from Inner Space*, says Shadow People are real, as are so many other paranormal entities. "I believe in all forms of 'spirit visitors'; incubi, succubi, poltergeists, Shadow People, ghosts – they are real," Gooch said. "But I do not think they are discarnate spirits, although I don't absolutely rule out that possibility."

Gooch, who has seen a Neanderthal materialize at a séance and made love with a succubi, still grounds these experiences in psychology. "They are creations and projections of our 'other mind' and brain," Gooch said. "But they do produce real, independent events in the real world."

As these entities thrust themselves into our lives, two forms emerge – benevolent and malevolent. Jack Allis said malevolent encounters far outweigh the benevolent ones because only one type is playing by the rules. "I definitely believe in a spirit world," Allis said. "What a spirit world is is just other dimensions. The reason the benevolent sprits aren't more active, it's an unwritten law of the universe not to interfere in the affairs of the indigenous people on the planet. The benevolent follow this, and the malevolent don't care. They're malevolent." Although Allis is convinced some of these spirit visitors are evil, he won't go so far as to call them demons. "I don't put a whole lot of credence in the traditional Christians," he said. "There's a right way to practice Christianity and a wrong way to practice Christianity. The wrong way… those people tend to see demons anywhere."

D.H. Parsons, president of The Bliss-Parsons Institute of Metaphysics in Columbia, Missouri, investigates hauntings and has encountered Shadow People more than once. "Both I and several of our investigators have seen these beings on investigations," Parsons said. "There are several theories as to what these are," including ghosts and, yes, demons. "In Christian interpretation – according to some paranormal investigators who happen to be Christian – some believe them to be a demon, or some sort of evil entity," Parsons said. "Who knows? My own feeling is that a Shadow Person is another representation of a residual memory of a person who had such a strong personality in life – good or bad – that a bit of their energy remained here in this dimension after their spirit crossed over."

This left over energy, Parsons said, is caught in a "loop" and replays over and over again. And, he added, he hasn't personally had a negative encounter with a Shadow Person. "In all of the investigations I have done I have never had any experience of a bad nature – no physical or spiritual attacks of any kind. Most of the time the spirit beings are either friendly to us, or confused by us, or curious as to why we are there. But they have never done us any harm, not even the Shadows."

Although many more people have encountered the malevolent Shadows (see Chapters 8 and 9), Debbie has encountered a benevolent Shadow Man. In 2000, she was lying awake in bed when pain bit her deeply. "Suddenly my head hurt horribly for no apparent reason," she said. "I was in a state that I cannot describe except to say that I was experiencing de-realization to some degree."

Corresponding with her pain, three balls of light "about the size of a 21-inch television set" appeared in the room. "I 'felt' someone tell me that they were 'his' protection and do not get up," she said. "I was then prompted to turn my head toward my closet and standing in front of it, as well at the foot of my bed, was the figure of what appeared to be an older man."

Although she couldn't see features, she knew this darker-than-night Shadow, highlighted by lights that were not from her room, was a man. "Lights were what formed his shape," she said. "As well as the prominent Shadow, the man was nothing more than lights or energy of some kind.

"Again, I felt someone tell me that he was a wise man just visiting to see how I am," she said. "I could move my head and eyes around the room with no disruption as to the location of what I was seeing. I just continued to stare at it for about 15 minutes and never got up because 'another' was keeping me from wanting to do so and so out of respect I just sat there and looked."

Eventually, the Shadow Man and the lights disappeared, and with them went her headache. "Now here's the real eerie part," Debby said. "I was in the coffee aisle of the store and glanced over at a box of green tea and the shape of the man that I had seen was the same shape of the individual on the box whose name is Kang. It was on a Good Earth green tea package. Being one that deals with much synchronicity in their life, I accepted the experience as a change of lifestyle so I put my coffee back and bought tea."

Demons of Christianity

Tonya and her family moved into their new house in 2005. New house, new neighborhood – and new visitors. It was nothing they'd expected. "I have seen a Shadow Person run by me more than once," Tonya said, and she wasn't alone. "My son has seen a black orb with smoke on it in his closet and the dog with him went crazy with fear."

But the thing that appeared to Tonya's daughter was

terrifying. "My daughter woke up and there was a thing looking at her," Tonya said. "The Shadow had pointed ears, large eyes with no pupils, the eyes had blood veins running down to where the pupil should have been."

The thing vanished, but the encounter was enough for Tonya's family. "I have had the house blessed and did a ritual cleansing but we still see activity," she said. "We all hear things in the closets and they have sliding doors and sometimes open by themselves."

Bishop James Long, pastor of St. Christopher Old Catholic Church in Louisville, Kentucky, has studied demonology and the paranormal for years, and knows stories like Tonya's are real. "Shadow People must be taken seriously and they can be quite dangerous," he said. "Quite often, when a human spirit tries to manifest itself, its form is black, or otherwise known as Shadow. It is energy trying to manifest itself so that it can appear to have the physical characteristics it had when living on earth."

These entities can move, communicate, and physically attack. "Certainly Shadows that attack are demonic in nature and should be avoided at all times," Long said. "I would strongly encourage anyone who witnesses a dark Shadow to be careful. It could be a human spirit trying to manifest itself, but it could also be demonic in nature."

How, then, can you tell which Shadows are spirits and which are evil?

David grew up in a house in Junction City, Kansas – a house with a dark, dark past. "The only thing I was told about the history was that the former owner's son was into the occult and Satanism," David said. "The walls had to be scrubbed because there were satanic symbols on the walls."

And in this house, David saw Shadow People. "There were a man and a woman on my bedroom wall across from my bed," he said. "They were there almost every night."

The outlines of the couple looked to be dressed in the

style of the 1940s. "They looked as if they were conversing," he said, "and would occasionally stop and look over at me while I was falling asleep." These Shadow figures didn't frighten David, but he never knew if the entities were good, or evil.

"There is always a way to find out if you are dealing with an evil entity," Long said. "Should you see an apparition of what appears to be a human spirit, there will always be some type of defect if it is demonic in nature." Only true human spirits, he said, can manifest themselves to the exact detail as to when they existed on Earth. "Remember, demonic entities will try to trick you and appear as a loved one that passed," Long said. "But when you view the entity, you will notice that the entity will have a flaw."

Has there been an insurgence of demonic activity in recent years?

Stephan Jansen of London thinks there has, and it's because of the breakdown of faith in society. "The problem we are facing in the UK at the moment is mainly due to the fact that society does not have faith in any God anymore," he said. "Money, jobs, etc., have taken over in people's lives, and God does not feature or fit in anymore."

Jansen feels the Church is largely to blame for this. "The Church in itself is growing weaker … allowing things that the Bible outrightly states is wrong," he said. "Binge drinking, drug abuse and sexual perversion – to name but a few – are getting worse, and these things take your mind to a different level of consciousness that you cannot control in the state you are in."

Once this happens, Jansen said, a person's spiritual defenses are gone, "and you are like a big, red tour bus just waiting for demons and evil spirits to board." These entities, he said, are Shadow People. "My guess is that the so-called Shadow People are nothing but a certain type of demon that finds it easier to cross over into our world. Although some seem to be oblivious of the fact that they are here, indicating that a window has somehow mistakenly been opened or left open into their dimension."

The Jinn of Islam

In the world of Islam, a paranormal entity known as the Jinn, which the Western world has turned into the genie, is at its best indistinguishable from man, and is at its worst our predator. "Jinns are invisible entities believed in by most all Muslims and Middle Eastern folklore," religion expert, Dashti Namaste said. "Jinns get in and out of human spheres regularly, and it is believed that any human is able to make 'contact' with a Jinn."

Taken from the Arabic root-word "Janna," meaning "to hide," the Jinn can become invisible, or change its form to appear as anything – man, animal or plant. Allah created the Jinn from "smokeless flame of fire" before creating man and bestowed powers upon the Jinn to test their loyalty to Him. Flying, teleportation, shape shifting, invisibility, and the ability to possess humans are some of those powers. Jinn who are Muslim rarely use their abilities for harm and can even marry and have children with human women.

Jinn who are non-Muslim are considered evil and warriors in the army of Shaytan, the devil. The non-Muslim Jinn are dangerous and considered "wicked." These Jinn appear as dark figures and often lurk in ruins, cemeteries, market places, and deserts waiting for an unsuspecting human soul to stumble in their midst. The wicked Jinn, much like the demons of the Christian world, are great deceivers and may present themselves as the ghost of a loved one to insert themselves into a human's life.

The good news about Jinn is they can be banished through prayer. The bad news – at least for non-Muslims – is a Jinn is attached to every one of us. When a non-Muslim dies, the Jinn will sit on their grave and curse them until Judgment Day.

The Wandering Souls of Hinduism

Although there are many prominent *sampradayas* (denominations) of the Hindu religion of India, and a great diversity in belief and practice within these sampradays, the concept of the *Antarloka* – the dimension between worlds where souls wander from incarnation to incarnation or when people are asleep – is held by many Hindus. And, from Antarloka comes a paranormal entity that corresponds to the description of Shadow People.

"In Hindu theology, there are unseen worlds beyond the physical world called the Antarloka and the Sivaloka," Suhag A. Shukla, interim Managing Director of the Hindu American Foundation said. "The Antarloka, which is closest to our world, is where souls live in between births in their astral bodies. It is possible for some of these souls to appear in our world in this astral form. What is being described here as a 'Shadow Person' would, in Hindu thinking, likely be the wandering soul of a person who died an untimely death and is earthbound for a period of time."

These souls in their astral forms can be simply lost, either wandering about in a daze or agitated. "For a person sensitive to their presence, they would be quite upsetting," he said. "Possession is possible, if rare, and can be dealt with by a Hindu priest."

Unseen Realms of Buddhism

In the world of Buddhism – an eastern Asia religion that focuses on peace and an austere way of life – dark Shadows exist just beyond our periphery; entities within our reach we shouldn't touch.

"There are many living beings existing in realms not seen by the average person," Rev. Heng Yuen of the online journal of Buddhism, *Dharma Bliss,* said. "But it [is] better to spend time studying the Buddha's teachings than probing into the Dark Shadows."

Yes, these "Dark Shadows" exist, said Alex Wilding,

an Oxford-educated expert in Tibetan Buddhism who runs a Buddhist center in the UK. But they can be dealt with. "Tibetan Buddhism is rich in dark, threatening entities," he said. "The teaching is that although they really do exist 'out there,' they only affect us through the power of our true demons: hatred, stupidity, pride, grasping, envy." These "personal demons," however, can be controlled. "They can be defeated by 1) appealing to something better, like the Buddha of compassion 2) fearlessness and 3) abandoning hatred, stupidity, pride, grasping and envy."

Native American Shamanism

Centuries prior to the expansion of Western culture, indigenous peoples worldwide learned and practiced metaphysics, much of which has been lost, or ignored. Allis feels many of the truths man seeks lie in these cultures. "Native American spirituality – it hasn't been contaminated," he said. "All the indigenous cultures from around the planet [knew the nature of life]. Western civilization is built on a mountain of lies."

And Shadow People? Yes, American Indians knew – and know – what these entities are. Wahde is Cherokee, and these Shadow Beings have a long and terrible history with the Cherokee people. "They're usually larger than an average person," Wahde said. "They're humanoid shaped, but not proportionate to a normal person. Their appearance is more monstrous in nature." Wahde should know, he's seen them.

According to Cherokee tradition, these Shadow Beings are the product of medicine people gone wrong. "There seem to be a classification of spiritual beings that are Shadow for the most part. These things can be manipulated by bad medicine or bad magic," Wahde said. "They either take that form to attack other people, or they use some other spiritual being as a spiritual attack."

These medicine people, Wahde said, have perverted the intended uses of their powers because of their own greed. "All creation is created for good, but with time it has been corrupted," he said. "To call it bad medicine, some even reject those terms. Medicine is used for good."

Medicine men once used their power over spirits or their power to take the form of foxes, wolves, owls, and Shadow People during warfare or to hunt – now they use it against one another, but at great sacrifice. "People who have used medicine that was one time used for good, they start to use that medicine to hurt other people for vengeance, to control," Wahde said. "At some point they lose their power and are parasitic and feed off others. They cease to be people and become something else."

The Cherokee refer to these dark medicine people as *sgili* (witch) whom you wouldn't notice passing on the street. "Yeah, or in Wal-Mart," Wahde said with a soft laugh. "They're still alive to some degree, but they're not necessarily considered human."

These Shadow People attacks range from physical attacks – which can target a specific body part like the heart or liver – to spiritual attacks. Although Wahde said older Cherokee don't like to speak about bad medicine, sgili, or Shadow People, the spiritual aspects of life aren't dangerous. "They're called superstitions, but a lot of people around here have personal experiences with these things and they're considered practical. For the most part, those spiritual things are not anything to worry about. The people are the problem."

Phillip Hensley, a Cherokee from Mexico, Missouri, has a more benevolent view of Shadow People than Wahde. "Shadow People are the deceased. They are deceased people," Hensley said. "They will make a very sudden appearance when you least expect it. I remember one elder telling me about Shadow People. If you ever have that feeling that someone is in the room, that's also

a Shadow Person." Hensley said Shadow People are part
of the belief system of the Anasazi, Hopi, Navajo, Apache
and many other Native American cultures.

Hensley has also had his own experience. "It was in
October 2003," he said. "I was at the – of all places – the
Natural History Museum in New York City." He was
standing in a section featuring artifacts from ancient
Mesoamerican Indian cultures, when he "heard a voice
inside of me," saying "do not take any pictures because
you are on sacred ground."

Hensley looked around for the source of the voice
and saw a Shadow Person he knew was an elderly Native
American woman. "I approached her and greeted her in
Cherokee," he said. "She would always avert her face
from me. She said nothing to me. I didn't hear it at all. It
was like a voice inside of me. That's in the Apache tradition. That's how these beings communicate. I just greeted
her and went away."

Hensley hasn't told many people about this encounter; he considers it a gift. "I took [the experience] as a
meaning that I was on the right path," he said. "I don't
really talk about it very much. It's just something I hold
very special."

Ghosts

Pauline Allred, a researcher for the Native American
Osage Indian Tribe, was lying quietly, preparing for sleep,
when she saw something in the light pouring into the
room from the hallway – and the something moved. "I
was going to sleep at home on a couch," she said. "[When]
it appeared near the top of my head."

The black figure she felt to be a man moved slowly as
she watched, then she grabbed for it. "I reached to touch
what appeared to be a hand reaching for me," Allred said.
"It vanished." But she knows the dark hand may come
back. "They are entities and appear suddenly when you

least expect them."

Carrie Hebert and Pat Murray, co-founders of Paranormal Researchers of Ohio, have investigated hauntings since 1983, and place many reports of Shadow People into the realm of misidentification. "Due to the positioning of rods and cones in the eye, things seen 'out of the corner of your eye' can appear as shadows," they said. "Also, things that are seen near the blind spot can be construed as wispy or half-formed. That would explain a lot of claims of people seeing ghosts, shadows, or Shadow People."

Those explanations don't account for all Shadow People encounters, however. "We do believe that there are 'things' known as Shadow People," they said. "Contrary to popular belief, they are not always evil or malicious, although inhuman [demonic] entities do often appear as very large, very dark, solid shadowy masses."

But a bulk of the reports not related to physical explanations could be ghosts. "Ghosts have to go through a metamorphosis of sorts to materialize," they said. "Sometimes we see the whole person, sometimes just half of a body, and sometimes we see them as a Shadow. It has to do with the amount of energy they are able to obtain in order to materialize."

Paranormal investigators like Alexandra Gargiulo, daughter of the ghost researcher Hans Holzer, and Linda Zimmermann, also an author and ghost hunter, agree ghosts may account for a number of Shadow People encounters. Shadow People walking through a house (or occasionally outdoors) like they have a destination, but pay no heed to the person who observes them, are probably earth-bound spirits. "These are ghosts once called Stay-Behinds by my father and are impressions of once was," Gargiulo said. "They mean no harm and a good medium can help them cross but not always."

Zimmerman has seen Shadow People and views them as something a little more ominous. "Based on interviewing witnesses and my own experiences, I don't consider Shadow People to be anything more than ghosts that are simply appearing in a dark form," she said, making a point that, since she's talking about ghosts, she doesn't like using the term Shadow People. "I've found no behavior or circumstances with a shadowy figure that goes beyond the 'normal paranormal.' If there is any distinction, it does seem as if the darker apparitions are connected to more negative hauntings."

Zimmerman saw her Shadow Person while investigating a haunting; a woman was renting a house and kept encountering a negative, dark figure. "During my investigation I saw something solid moving through the living room blocking the dim light coming through the curtains..." Zimmerman said. "It turns out the man who built the house was a nasty character who liked to victimize women, and died of cancer in the house."

Although most Shadow People encounters seem harmless, there are plenty of occasions where these encounters turn negative – very negative.

CHAPTER 4

Benign Shadows

The most common Shadow Man report has him walking through someone's home oblivious to the people occupying the house. These Shadow People move through a room, or down a hallway, paying no heed to the frightened humans left in their wake. Jim and Angie Stone-Dornbrook of Independence, Missouri, have often seen this type of Benign Shadow in their home.

Angie believes that this Shadow Person is related to her. "My grandfather who died in 2000 is at my house often," she said. "He appears as a Shadow in my kitchen [and] in the bedroom." Like all the benign reports of Shadow People, this Shadow walks through the Dornbrook home and, most disturbing to Jim, visits their bedroom. "I can tell he's there even when he doesn't show himself," Angie said. "I can smell his Chesterfield cigarettes. Jim can sense him as well – it creeps him out. Jim made me tell [the entity] he could no longer go on his side of the bed because the smell of smoke made him think the house was on fire."

The Rhine Research Center's Sally Rhine Feather said spirits are a logical explanation for these Benign Shadows because of the large number of eyewitness accounts. "[Many] believe that some type of consciousness exists beyond death and sort of remains in certain locations," she said. "Many after-death encounter reports in all cultures raise the possibility of spirit survival, especially in well-documented cases where apparitions of apparently departed people are seen by several people and/or animals with reactions...Some studies have found mediums [who can] pick out certain spots independently of field investigators and that helps suggest that something is there – is it a spirit, a type of energy, or persistence of effect over time?"

Omens

The television show went to commercial. In the brief second between the program and commercial, when the screen went black, Omega (online name) saw something on the screen – a man.

"I saw the silhouette of a person standing outside my door, as it was partially open," Omega said. "I turned my head to see who was at the door, but no one was there." She left the couch and tried to find the source of the reflection, but found nothing. When her program resumed, she started watching television again.

"I kept seeing [the figure] every time the screen went to black," she said. "It got my curiosity to see what was making this figure." She turned off the television and the figure was still on the screen – looking at her house. "I put my face to the set, turned 180 degrees to see where the reflection was coming from. It was coming from outside."

Omega could make out a telephone pole about 20 feet away on the sidewalk. "It looked as if it was standing directly in front of the pole," she said. "After trying to figure out why I was seeing this strange shape of a person whose outline of shoulder, arms, legs, and torso I could make out, I gave up and shut the door."

Omega forgot about the figure until she drove home from work the next day and saw an ambulance parked across the street. "The old lady who lived there had died," Omega said. "I started to think that perhaps that shadow figure wasn't watching me, but her. Her house was visible in the reflection the day earlier being just across from where I lived. [When] a new family moved in, I never had that experience with the TV again – I moved it." Was Omega's Shadow Man foretelling her neighbor's death?

Although most cultures have different omens – crows, adders, even overturned shoes – Shadow People are one of the American Indian omens. An anonymous poster on "From The Shadows" called my attention to the Shadow Sisters: "I am Native American and live in San Luis Valley Colorado … Shadow People have always been part of our lives. What about the Three Shadow Sisters (Death); has anyone out there seen them?"

Many people have, said Brad Steiger, the author of *Shadow World* and many other books on the paranormal. "Sherry [Brad's wife] and I follow many of the essential concepts and cosmology of Native American shamanism," he said. "Shadow People are well known to traditional native people and in almost all instances their appearance presage either the approach of death or negative destined circumstances."

Years ago while speaking at a gathering of the Plains and tribes, Steiger, an adopted Seneca of the Wolf Clan, discovered that those who have experienced Shadow People don't take them lightly. "After my appearance on 'Coast to Coast,' [a late-night paranormal radio talk show] I received a number of emails chiding me for not speaking more about Shadow People," he said. "'You know who they are,' I was scolded."

Priscilla Wolf – known as Little Butterfly – is an Apache medicine woman and artist. She approached Steiger about "The Three Sisters," Shadow People who foretell approaching doom. "The Three Sisters [are] all Shadow People who appear during death or [as a] warning," she wrote in an email to Steiger. "My son has seen them in Albuquerque years back. I have seen them walking on a Sandia Mountain dirt road." The sisters, which legend has died tragically at the hands of their family, appear to the doomed as identical walking Shadows. "They walk alike, look alike and walk on air," Little Butterfly wrote. "In Grants, New Mexico, at one of the Indian grave sites, they come out to greet their loved ones that die."

Shadows Night After Night

Shadows have always been part of Danny's life, from the first home he remembers to the one he and his family live in now. "I was only about seven when we moved from the house but I remember very well what I would see night after night," Danny said. "People all shapes and sizes walking down our hallway – just Shadows."

Day after day he looked for the source of these Shadows, "to try and explain what I was seeing and never finding one." Now, as an adult, Danny and his family live in a different house, but the visitors are the same. "My son says he sees people walking down the hall, and he has requested his door be shut," Danny said. "I am inclined to believe him because of my past experience it sounds very much the same."

Being in the military, Danny moves his family often and has never been rid of these specters. "We have lived with paranormal before," he said. "Dark figures walking up stairs and standing out in our yard, things going bump in the night. My son has never been afraid. He would just say our house was haunted, almost proud, but here is different. We have not yet lived here a year and he is afraid to go to sleep."

Shadows All Her Life

Young Maggie Antone was lying in bed in a Cleveland, Ohio, suburb, staring through the darkness of her room into the lighted hall, when she realized she was not alone.

"I noticed the silhouette of a very tall man in my doorway, in what looked like a position that was leaning against the doorframe," she said. "I particularly noticed the outline of a turned up jacket collar, like he/it was wearing a heavy leather coat. I, thinking it was my father, turned to greet the figure and it was gone."

Maggie often saw this Shadow Man in her periphery, always disappearing as she turned to face it. "Another common sighting was a Shadowy figure with what looked like a very unkempt head of hair," she said. "As I was sitting in our living room watching TV, I saw this Shadowy figure walk across the length of the room from the corner of my vision, and, as usual, [it] disappeared when I looked straight at it."

But, the Shadow Man didn't always disappear. "At one point in my childhood I had bunk beds in my room," she said. "I was sleeping on the top bunk one night, and for some reason I went to look over the side of my bed." Someone was already there.

"I came face to face with the messy-haired Shadow Man," she said. "It seemed like it was coming up to look over the top of the bed at me, and we sort of collided. I jumped back really quickly in surprise, and it was gone."

Although most of Maggie's encounters occurred while she was a child, she's seen the messy-haired Shadow Man all her life. Now that she's an adult, the encounters are fewer – but the Shadows are still there. "I was living at home while I finished my graduate coursework, and one evening I was lying in bed and happened to open my eyes to see a full silhouette standing in the middle of the room," she said. "I immediately sat up in surprise, and it was gone. It was already quite dark in my room, but the figure was easy to pick out because it was a more intense shade of darkness – which is the best way I can think of to describe it."

In 2006, Maggie was packing for a weekend trip, when she saw the Shadow Man for the last time. "It was the most intriguing and unsettling experience I had in that house," she said. Maggie had walked down the basement steps to the laundry room and passed by the recreation room where her younger brother and his friends had been sleeping. "I wasn't sure if they were still down there or not, but as I came to find out, I was alone in the house," she said.

But as she walked by the recreation room, something in the room moved. "I saw a Shadow on the floor, which looked to be caused by someone moving around in the rec room," she said. "I called out to let my brother and his friends know it was just me coming down, but when I got to the bottom of the stairs, turned left into the room, no one was in there."

Passing off the experience as a product of her imagination, she turned and continued to the laundry room – but the Shadow was there again. "I saw another Shadow on the floor through the door into the laundry room, which made it look like someone was retreating into that room away from me," she said. "The only thing I could think was that it was one of my [brother's] friends who was still in his PJs and didn't want me to see him, so I called out again saying it was just me."

When she followed this retreating Shadow into the laundry room, she found … nothing. "There was no living thing in the laundry room," she said. And there was no other way out. Standing in the laundry, looking at the bare room, fear engulfed her. "There was no way out of the laundry except the way I came in," she said. "At that point, I became a bit rattled since I knew what I saw, had verbally addressed it, and found nothing." Maggie grabbed her laundry, ran upstairs, and went to the telephone. "I called a friend to tell him what happened," she said. "Otherwise I would have felt crazy."

The Cold Room

The house in South Euclid, Ohio, was built in the early years after World War I. It was a Sears Modern Home, a mail-order house popular before the Great Depression. Nobody lived in the house long, and, during the years between 1967 and 1975, Lisa Falour discovered why.

"The house had already had numerous owners and changed hands often," Lisa said. "It always felt creepy to me." Repairs were seemingly endless, especially the roof. It always leaked. But what bothered Lisa's family most was the cold. "It was impossible to keep the place warm enough in winter, and Ohio winters by Lake Erie are deadly nasty," she said. "The family room was the kitchen, as it was usually the only warm place in the whole house. Even when the living room chimney was lit, what little heat we had ran up the flue."

The cold continued in Lisa's bedroom; it was the coldest room in the house and she usually did her school-work in the kitchen. "I spent quiet evenings at the kitchen table, doing my homework. It was impossible to study in [my room]," she said. But from the kitchen, she could see unwelcomed visitors – black human shapes cut from the fabric of the dimly lighted dining room.

"I constantly saw Shadow People walking around in the dining room while I sat at the kitchen table," she said. "They were normal sized and silent, and though usually out of the corner of my eye, when looked at straight, they would just quietly move on. It wasn't a trick of the eye."

When she turned on the dining room light, the brightness drove these Shadows from the room. "They annoyed me, but it's hard to know what to do about such a thing," Lisa said. "I spoke to my mother about the Shadow People, and she just calmly said, 'well, maybe the place is haunted. If they don't hurt you, don't worry about them too much.'"

Lisa moved from the house on Telhurst Road when she turned 18, "and never lived there again." She would stay with her parents on short visits, again seeing the Shadows that walked in the dining room. "I never heard a sound from the Shadow People, and didn't feel particularly threatened, but I did feel uneasy and not happy they were there," she said. "It made me not like the house. All I can say is the house was creepy."

My Dog Chased a Shadow

Paul was working in his back yard when he glanced through the sliding glass door at his pit bull terrier and saw the Shadow thing in his house. "I saw a black orb with a tail speed through my kitchen close to the ceiling," he said. "It made a u-turn and headed out the hallway where it came from."

Normally, Paul would have dismissed what he saw, but he wasn't the only one who saw it. "The whole time my dog Star was looking up at it and followed it with her eyes," he said. "She is a game little pit bull and immediately gave chase."

Paul ran inside and found Star running through the house, barking as if it was chasing an intruder. "This was not a reflection of some kind," Paul said. "Its image is burned in my head. It was smoky black, semi-transparent, and seemed to have a trail behind it. It moved with purpose, circling the room."

Star doesn't chase its tail, Paul said. He's convinced they both saw something – something that might often visit his house. "Sometimes in the night she will bolt from her sleep and run down the hall, without a peep," he said. "Then come back in a few minutes later after sitting in the dark at the head of my stairway. This has startled my wife and I a few times. Something is definitely going on."

The Lady in the Hall

The Shadows in the house didn't frighten Carrie. She was used to them. "There were two of them in an old house I lived in when I was a little girl back in the 1970s," she said. "One stayed in our hallway and she – it was female in shape and feel – would move in front of you and you would walk through her before you realized what you' were doing." Whenever Carrie walked through the Shadow Lady, she had to push through a layer of cold, and felt "a little ill" whenever it happened.

But the other Shadow, a man, wasn't so easy to deal with. "He would get mad at my mother when she moved the bedroom furniture around," she said. "It had to stay in a certain way or he would torment her or anyone else who slept in her bed until she moved the furniture back."

After Carrie's family moved from the house, owned by her grandmother, it was often empty. "My grandmother couldn't get anyone to stay longer than six months," she said. "Some of the people would just up and leave in the middle of the night. Can't say I blame them."

Carrie didn't see the Shadows until she was grown. "I saw them again when I was in the hospital having my daughter much too early," she said. "I died and they had to shock me to restart my heart." But, before Carrie was revived, she saw three Shadows standing at the foot of her bed. "The nurses and doctors walked right through them," she said. "I don't think anyone saw them but me. I had my daughter but she died shortly after. I didn't feel any evil from them, just that they were there for a purpose. Who knows what it was."

Christmas Shadow

Christmas morning 2006, a Shadows reader with the online name Londoner, was walking her dogs in the local park at 5:30 a.m. when she saw something move on the trail ahead of her. "I glanced at a tree about 50 yards ahead and saw something black, like an arm, move across it," she said. "This wasn't a big tree and its bare branches were literally touching a very bright lamp post a few feet away so it was well illuminated and too narrow for anyone to hide behind."

She kept moving down the trail, getting closer and

closer to the tree, and the black arm, when she noticed there were no nearby bushes or anything for someone – or something – to hide behind. "I was about 20 feet away when this jet black man shape scampered [counter] clockwise around the tree and disappeared," she said. "It was about 5 feet, 5 inches or less, and there was something inhuman about the way it moved."

The thing was uniformly pitch black "from head to toe" under the light of the lamp, she said. "The light didn't seem to have any effect on it. The only detail I could guess at from its shape was that it seemed to be wearing clothes. As its knees came up to scamper, its ankles weren't tapered, giving the impression of it wearing trousers. I walked all round that tree – at a safe distance. There was nobody there."

She Woke, Screaming

Shadow People torment Cliff, and he can't get rid of them. "I have been seeing things above me, over me, around me all times of the day, more often in the evening in the dark," he said. "This has been happening all my life."

Shadow People stand, sit or hover around Cliff's bed at night, black, human-shaped holes punched into the darkness of his room. "I first passed this off as night terrors," he said. "But when I started to see them and I knew I was awake things changed."

One night Cliff's girlfriend switched sides of the bed with him. She woke him screaming. "She had seen something crouched beside her on my side of the bed," Cliff said. "I had never told her that I see these things until that night. Now she won't sleep on that side anymore. I'm almost scared to tell her that they are on her side, too."

These walking Shadows visit Cliff almost every night, and he wants them to stop. "I have tried to attack them to no success," he said. "I have tried to talk to them with no success. I have even tried to make a deal with them. But it just doesn't happen and they do not go away. We need to figure out what is going on."

Swedish Shadow Man

Fatima-Zohraa Tribak was cooking dinner in her Stockholm apartment when she realized she was not alone. "It all started in the middle of the day," she said. "I tried to turn a lid that didn't want to open. I remember I was thinking, 'Now it would have been nice to have a strong man helping me.'"

The lid wouldn't budge. She placed the unopened can on the counter and started preparing something else. "I gave up trying to open the can and I turned my back on it," she said. "Then I heard 'click,' but I didn't care because I had something cooking on the stove. I just thought that it was the food cooking making the sound. And then I turned around and what I saw made me jump."

The lid was lying next to the can. "I thought it was a good helping spirit, so I said 'thank you' out loud," she said. "And then I felt stupid and started to try to think of a good natural explanation for what happened."

Later that evening, she was getting ready for sleep when her "good helping spirit" visited again. "I had been in the bathroom and was walking out. I turned the light out and started to walk towards my bedroom," she said. "For some reason I looked into a big mirror and I saw a Shadow shaped like a man. I thought to myself, 'what is making this Shadow look like this in the hall?'"

In the mirror, the Shadow was accompanied by a light…a light she had turned out. "I turned around and the light in the hall was still turned out, so there was nothing I could see there," she said. "I was still looking into the dark when I thought I must have been mistaken of what I saw."

She wasn't. "I turned around to go to my bed and I

looked into my big mirror again to make sure I was wrong from the start," she said, but what she saw terrified her. "There the light was and the man again. This time I ran into my bedroom and I jumped up on my bed shaking. I'm a 39-year-old woman, but I felt like a small girl at this moment."

She's seen the apparition since this encounter, "but this time it moved" – and, although the figure has never harmed her, she's worried it might. "I have tried to find out if this is something I should be scared of or if I can relax," she said. "I didn't know where I should go to ask someone without them thinking that I'm crazy. I feel quite silly. But in the same way I'm thinking, why should I feel silly? I really would like to know what this is. Is it something in my mind, or is it something real?"

Absorbed by Shadows

The apartment in Leighton Buzzard, a town 40 miles north of London, was only two years old when Adam Patterson moved in. It was typical: bedroom, bathroom, kitchen/dining area, and a living room spilling inside the front door. But, as normal as it looked, there was something strange about the apartment.

"Upon my first day there, I noticed the carpet was all worn out in front of where the TV goes, but I didn't think too much of it, only that it was a little bit odd," Adam said. "I also saw that a plug socket above the sink was hanging off. Again, I didn't think too much of it, but at first glance, I did question the reasons for this."

Adam's life in the apartment was "fine for the first few months." But that soon changed. "Despite being very low about certain aspects of my life, in regards to the actual flat, I was pleased," he said. "However, the past two months have been increasingly strange." Like the feeling of being watched every night.

Then there are the lights and Shadows. "Strange

lights appear whilst sitting on my couch in front of the TV, when I only had two small wall lights on, which are placed behind me at the kitchen area," he said. "A couple of strange Shadows would regularly appear and they would react to my movements when I decided to 'test' them."

And, by testing, Adam meant touching. For two months, Adam has kept the same schedule. He's spent every Thursday, Friday, Saturday, and Sunday night, sitting in front of the TV waiting for the lights and Shadows to appear. "[I turn] the TV off with the remote control, and look in the TV's reflection if I can find the source of these Shadows and lights," he said. "I have always been convinced that what I am searching for is behind me at the kitchen area."

For these two months, Adam has obsessively moved from the couch to the TV to gain a better view of the light and Shadow reflections on the screen. "Last week, I had an extremely interesting consideration dawn on me," he said. "I suddenly realized that for two months now – several times each week – I have been in the middle of experiencing these strange lights and Shadows, and ended up moving from my couch to sit in front of the TV in order to give a closer inspection to the screen's reflections." He thought, "I am probably going to start wearing out the carpet at this rate," when he realized the carpet between the couch and the television was already worn – probably by the previous occupant.

"This same night, I worked out that from the direction of light, together with the placement of each Shadow, the source of the disturbance was most definitely coming from the kitchen wall," he said. "'[Those people] next door have found a way to look at me through the wall,' I thought." He walked into the kitchen to try and find a gap where his next-door neighbor might be playing jokes on him, when he thought if he were doing the peeping, he'd unscrew the wall socket.

"Wow, another coincidence," he said, the wall socket in the kitchen already hanging loose. "This has perhaps already been done by someone else." Did the apartment's former tenant, he wondered, think and do exactly as he did? And if so, why?

"Saturday night I stayed in to watch TV and during the entire night I was experiencing a very strong feeling of being watched," he said. "The Shadows on the wall were looking more and more like human heads, and they were once again reacting to my movements."

Adam turned off the television and he saw a reflection on the television screen. "Two slightly distorted human silhouettes were sitting on either side of me," he said. "I also noticed my own silhouette was very unlike me; my head seemed a little larger than usual, and the reflection of my movements was often delayed or ahead of me."

He started playing games with the reflections, watching them move as he motioned toward them. Then he noticed something even more unnerving – one of the Shadows was nudging him closer to the other. "For the entire evening, one of them was attempting to lure me into the other one," he said. "I think it wanted to consume me somehow. I know this all sounds crazy, but I was in direct contact with two very real Shadow People."

Although Adam speculates the Shadow People are from a different dimension, he doesn't know this for certain. He only knows what he feels. "I don't think they are necessarily evil. I describe them as curious," he said. "But it's absolutely horrible for me."

A Visit to the "Zoo"

A Shadows reader who calls herself The Real Green Witch has been one with the paranormal for years, but didn't encounter the Shadow Man until she was pregnant in 2006. "I was heavily pregnant and coming out of the bath during the day [when I] turned to get my towel and came face-to-face with this six-foot Shadow Man," she said. "He was not see-through, even though it was daytime and was black from head to toe with no other features."

The Green Witch stood, dripping water onto the floor, watching the Shadow Man until he faded from sight – but he wasn't gone. "From then [on] I couldn't get rid of them," she said. "I have seen grayish small ones walk through my bedroom, black flying ones around my bedroom ceiling. Even when I'm not in there during the day, I was seeing this."

After she gave birth and brought her son home, the encounters became worse. "Every night there was a black hooded person with a sunken white face like an old man. He was bent over like an old man and he just used to watch us – sort of Reaper-like."

Unexplained flashing lights began to appear in the Green Witch's home and she found they were the harbinger of the Shadow Man. "The hooded figure came back," she said. "He stood beside my husband and looked into my son's cot, turned to look at me then disappeared through the bedroom wall. A few minutes later there was a white Shadow Person."

The white entity looked to her like a Shadow Person, but radiated a white light instead of darkness. "He came up to my son's cot, looked at it, then walked away," she said. "Then three groups of ten [dark Shadow People] walked up to my son's cot, looked in at him and walked away."

She, her son, and husband are healthy and happy, even though the Shadows continue to invade their lives. "I don't sense they are evil," she said. "I think they are here to help us, learn from us and watch us, sort of like a human zoo."

But others feel these entities are all too evil.

CHAPTER 5

Shadows of Terror

James Buckham has seen blacker-than-night Shadows, he has fought them, and he has won. "I am an exorcist, and have been doing this work successfully for a long time," Buckham said. "I am not a member of the clergy, nor a pagan. The method of exorcism I use was taught to me many years ago by people who helped me deal with a demonic haunting at my place of employment." This demonic haunting – marked by the appearance of a blob-like Shadow – was an event that changed Buckham's life.

Buckham worked as a baker in an old building in Fort Smith, Arkansas. He arrived early to make bread, and every morning would stand helplessly as something knocked pans and utensils from his hands. "I saw what looked like black clouds floating across the floor, and there was a feeling of outright evil," he said. "The occurrences followed me home as well to the point where I was scared to go to sleep, and felt as if I was fighting for my life."

Buckham contacted a psychic friend who, with the help of an exorcist, banished the demon from Buckham's life. "They not only cleared the place of all negative entities, but through them I learned to do the very same work," he said.

Shortly after the exorcism, Buckham left Arkansas and moved to Beverly, Massachusetts, where he now uses his skills to help others. "All my clients come to me by word of mouth," he said. "I do not charge for my services; my only desire is to help those in need."

In his work as an exorcist, Bucknam has seen many, many Shadow People and sees them for what they are. "Let's start with what they are not," he said. "They are not creations of over-active imaginations. They are not thought forms, nor are they deceased humans who have become something else."

Shadow People are negative spirits that come to our "plane of existence" through portals, or doorways that lead to places of great negativity, he explained. "These doorways can be found everywhere, and unfortunately can only be opened if someone of their free will chooses to."

And that's when the trouble begins. "When Shadow People invade a home or harass someone, many things happen over time," he said. A person's health begins to deteriorate, their home develops a chill that never seems to go away, they get little – if any – sleep and are tortured by their dreams. "Many other occurrences take place as well, and the goal throughout this is to bring fear, hopelessness, and pain to that person's life," Bucknam said. "This sets off an energy that these Shadow People enjoy. They change the atmosphere of a place to an energy that they are more comfortable with. This energy is very unhealthy, and over time makes for a toxic home."

These Shadows of negative energy are common and will make your life hell.

Voices in the Dark

The air at the California ranch was calm the night Darren Hullstrunk took a group of friends to his family's property near Fresno. The calmness didn't last. "We've all heard, seen, felt something in this ranch house and heard all the stories from the parents and how scared they have gotten," he said. Darren and friends who've been at the ranch before – Brittany, Audrey, Mike, Mark, and Mike's brother Richie – pulled down the drive and arrived at the ranch house on the evening of June 22, 2008. The night had started to cool, but the trip, to this point, was normal.

"Audrey, Richie and I went for a walk and we went the same route the walk always goes," Darren said. "We got back to the house and we all stood outside because it was cooler than the house was."

Richie sensed something was wrong, but nobody realized that – yet. "Richie zoned out and stared at a large dog statue for almost a good five to 10 minutes," Darren said. "It wasn't 'til Mark had moved the statue that Richie snapped out of it and looked behind him. He didn't know what happened."

Hungry, the group moved inside and discussed dinner. The women volunteered to go to the grocery store. "As they left, Richie suddenly sprung up and pulled up a blind and just stared outside," Darren said. "Mike moved his finger in the way and Richie just pulled it down." Darren ran outside and looked in the direction Richie was staring but saw nothing out of the ordinary. He could, however, still see Richie staring out the window.

"His head went to an angle as if he was following something, but nothing was there," Darren said. He went back inside and everyone was now looking out the window. "Mike opened the blinds fully and we all looked out and saw nothing."

Then Richie told them what he'd seen. "Richie said he saw a Shadow that ran towards the car," Darren said, "but didn't know if it followed the [women] or went into the grape vineyard or the other side of the road."

As the men sat around the living room, Richie "zoned out" again. "This time as if he was trying to write out something with his finger," Darren said. "He snapped out and didn't remember a thing."

They called Richie's family to pick him up but didn't know the depth of Richie's fear until he got on the telephone. "As he was talking on the phone they told him to say a prayer over and over," Darren said. "After the first time he said it, he got a headache and said he couldn't say it again. He started crying and saying he has to get out of here, it's going to get him. What it was, Richie didn't say, but when they walked Richie outside to Mike's car, he panicked.

"Richie started freaking out," Darren recalled. "'It's out here, it's going to get me,' he went on." Darren looked around them, but saw nothing.

Mike took Richie home and as soon as they drove off the property, Richie felt better, but he couldn't remember anything that had happened. Before he left, however, Richie told everyone about the voices. "He said if he didn't leave, [the Shadow] was going to kill all of us, and it didn't want him or Mike there," Darren said. "Richie told Mike he was hearing two voices, the evil one and another one telling him how to counter the evil. He made Mike promise to leave a light on."

By the time Mike and Richie left, Audrey and Brittany had returned. After supper, Darren and Audrey went outside. "We had noticed [earlier] there was no moon outside and no clouds with only a few stars," he said. "When Mike got back there was a moon and it was blood red."

Although, unnerved, Darren is fascinated by the encounter. "I'm going to be checking the area for sightings," he said. "I want to see if I can find out what happened."

It Looms Over My Bed

Katie moved into her fourth floor dorm room the Friday before Fall 2007 classes at her university began. "When I first moved in, it was really damp in the room and it had a different smell to it," she said. "An old smell."

A friend, Harrison, noticed the smell, too. "He said, 'it's a fragrance,'" Katie said. "It wasn't my perfume. I didn't know if it was something or nothing."

For the first week in her new room, it was nothing. The second week, she realized something else was with her. "I felt a presence in my room," Katie said. "It's almost oppressive. The feeling I get [is] I just feel tense all the time. When I feel the presence, I start looking over my shoulder a lot. It's hard to go to sleep."

Katie sees things in the corner of her eyes – things that move and vanish when she turns to face them. She sleeps with covers up to her neck. "It's a guy. It's a Shadow peering over the side of my bed," she said. "It's a loft bed so you'd have to be as tall as the room. It was just dark, but it was definitely a form. I could see eyes, nose, mouth. I just couldn't see the details. All I know is it's a guy and I don't know what he wants. I don't want to piss it off. I don't want to talk with it. I just want to coexist. I don't like to talk about what's going on when I'm in my room. I hate the dark."

Bedroom Watchers

Something jumped on Kaitlin Straub's bed. Straub, 16, of Marceline, Missouri, stirred and looked at the clock – it was 2:30 a.m.

"I've always been a little sensitive to the paranormal and because of that I am a light sleeper," she said. "I woke up early one morning because I felt something on the bed."

The family had two dogs and a cat, so Straub's first instinct was to shoo the animals away – but there were no animals in her room. "At first I thought nothing of it," she said. "However, I rolled over and crouched on the foot of the bed was, what I describe, as a Shadowy figure."

She started to get out of bed, but she saw more human Shadows dot her room. "I realized there were several Shadow People scattered around my room," she said. "I started to panic. I felt dizzy so I covered my face with my pillow, [and] moments later my mom turned on the light and asked why I was screaming at 6 o'clock in the morning?"

Straub's eyes darted around the room, but the Shadow People were gone – and so had the time. "Three and a half hours had passed and I know for a fact I wasn't screaming," she said.

So what happened?

Kaitlin Straub's brother, paranormal investigator Ryan Straub, now of Centralia, Missouri, once lived in that house and said odd occurrences there are common. "Other haunted phenomenon has occurred there," he said. "Children's voices outside late at night when no children were present. Poltergeist activity: doors slamming, windows breaking, lights/TV/radio going on and off. Monstrous figures and Shadow People."

Ryan Straub, who also studies the protective properties of totems, candles, incense, and other Native American, Old World, and Wiccan traditions, has helped his sister keep the Shadows at bay. "I was very panicky," Kaitlin Straub said. "I now use protective measures to prevent Them from happening again."

It Mocks Me

Billy encountered his first Shadow Person on a ghost hunt with friends. The dark, male figure slowly stepped in front of him. "It almost comes to a stop, looks at me, and walks off," Billy said. "The thing that caught my attention is that it was all black, but I could still tell it had clothing on, and its eyes, they were a sharp, almost glowing red." Then it simply walked away.

Unfortunately, this encounter with a Shadow Man was not Billy's last. "I really never wanted to see one again," Billy said. "There was something very unpleasant about him, but I cannot say what it is." Shortly after his first encounter, Billy started seeing Shadow People more often. "As I was sitting in the back seat of a car, I saw a man at a bus stop," Billy said. "He had one of these Shadow People behind him. The Shadow Person was mocking him, making fun of him and doing anything to get his, or my, attention. It was just plain weird."

Billy still sees these human-mocking Shadow People, but worse for Billy, he knows they see him. "I continued to see Shadow People this way," he said. "They are almost always with a person, following them, and they must know I can see them because, like I said, they always try to get my attention. Are they demons, or some other evil?"

Feeling of Doom

In the summer of 2006, Dan and Blaine spent the night at a friend's house. "We slept on the couches in the living room," Dan said. "Midway through the night I woke up with a feeling I can only describe as doom because it was more than terror." Dan lay frozen on the couch, wondering what was happening.

"Unknowing why I feel this way, Blaine asks me if I was awake." Blaine felt the terror, too. This feeling of dread drifted off, only to creep back upon them later when they heard something they couldn't identify. "The same feeling of doom came over us," Dan said. "We were quiet for a few minutes, but I still could not sleep. A bit into this, I heard Blaine whisper, 'Dan.'"

Dan opened his eyes and saw the silhouette of a man in the living room's bay window. "He was walking in our direction," Dan said. "I blinked and it was still there." The hulking, black figure wasn't Blaine, or the man whose house they were staying in. "By the time the figure walked out of sight of the bay window, I reached for my cell phone and opened the light onto the room."

No one else was in the room and Dan saw the area where this figure had just walked in blocked by an ottoman. They spent the rest of the night outside. "An important factor is what the feeling is exactly," Dan said. "It's not like fear or nervousness that you get when the hairs stand on the back of your neck. It's a much more intense feeling of doom or dread. It's a negative energy in the air like when you walk in on two people after an argument; you can kind of feel the negative energy in the air. But much, much, much, more negative and intense."

My Aunt's House

Debbie's husband heard their daughter cry out in the night. He woke Debbie, telling her he was going to bring their daughter to bed with them. It was a house strange to the girl; they were staying the night with Debbie's aunt for the first – and last – time.

"We had never stayed the night at my aunt's house, but for some strange reason we ended up staying there," Debbie said. "When my husband attempted to pick our daughter up, he felt someone standing next to him." He thought it was one of Debbie's cousins who had also heard their daughter and had come to help. But all he could see was a Shadow in the night. He spoke his daughter's name, but the black figure was silent.

Then the terror began. "When he attempted to pick up our daughter, he couldn't move," Debbie said. "He called for me to turn on the light, but I could not move. The tone of his voice was really scaring me." Debbie yelled for her aunt and uncle, but no one heard her. "Then my husband yells for me to pray to our Father," Debbie said. "As soon as I finished praying, I yelled out for my aunt again, then she responded."

After Debbie's prayer, the black Shadow was gone and they could move again.

Frozen with Fear

Paula Peedro was a child in the early 1970s when she was introduced to something dark and evil. "I was kneeling on the floor by my bed in the dark praying," she said. "As I gazed into the corner, perhaps four feet away, I could see a dark human form walking towards me from a great distance."

The shape was much blacker than the darkness of her room and appeared to grow as it approached her. "The figure started out small and kept getting bigger and bigger," Peedro said. "I was filled with a profound sense of dread and the certainty that I would die if the figure got close enough."

Fear rooted her to the kneeling position next to the bed, her eyes bolted onto this blacker-than-night figure. "I was frozen from fright but eventually managed to break my gaze and turn on the light," she said, "when, of course, the figure disappeared." But Paula knows the terrible Shadow she saw that night in the darkness was real, and it fed off her fear.

The Shadows Follow Me

Mark was 10 the first time he saw a Shadow Person. He, his sister, and his mother had fallen asleep in their living room watching movies. A sound like plastic bags rustling pulled him from sleep. "As soon as I sat up and looked toward the front door where [the noise] had come from, I heard a few voices say 'Shhh...'"

Three Shadows of tall, broad men stood in the room, looming over his family. "They had no detail. They were just an absence of light," he said. "One of them whispered my name and said, 'we are going to kill you.'" Fear consumed him. He tried to wake his mother and sister; he shook them and shouted at them, but they wouldn't move. When he turned back toward the Shadows, they were gone, but not for long.

"I have since seen them again and again; most were in that same house, but I still see them outside, in other houses, other buildings," he said. "I have a sense that the ones I still see are the same ones I first saw, that they follow me specifically, though I don't know why. They make me feel terrified, sometimes beyond the capacity for any kind of action. I'm not sure, but I think there is some reason they aren't allowed to harm me, but I sense that they want to. They are so angry."

Tessa's Shadow

It was about 8 p.m. and nine-year-old Tessa was in her brother's room. He lay on his bed reading a book, and Tessa stood at the window, looking into their family garden, when she felt something was wrong.

"I can still remember it as if it was yesterday," Tessa, now an adult, said. "Suddenly I got this feeling like I was standing in an electric field. I don't know, like a soft vibrating."

Whatever was happening to Tessa left her unable to breathe. "I turned around to face the room again, and all of a sudden I see this Shadow moving from the left side of the room towards the wall," she said. Somehow, she immediately knew it was male. "He had the strangest way of walking, like he was trying to sneak up on someone or sneak away from something. I felt he was no friendly being, and then he was gone; just went through the wall."

Her brother, facing the opposite wall, didn't see it, or feel the same electric field as Tessa. "When it was gone and I could breathe again, I gasped out to my brother if he didn't see that guy, but he just thought I was nuts," she said.

I'm Stuck in This Place

A month after Carli moved into a large, three-room apartment alone, save for her children on weekends, something in the apartment made itself known. "The night before I was supposed to get my kids, I was watching TV," Carli said. "All of a sudden it was turning on and off, channels going up and down, as well as the volume. I thought I was sitting on the remote until I looked over on the stand next to where I was sitting, there it was."

She took the batteries out of the remote in case there was an electric short in the device, but the TV was still changing channels and volume. "I unplugged it and went to go try to get some sleep in the other room." The electronics in her apartment behaved themselves until her children came to visit for the weekend.

"That weekend my two boys were already asleep and my daughter was staying up late watching Animal Planet when the fan started changing speeds." The box fan went from fast to slow and on to off. "We both freaked out over it, and went into the boys room and fell asleep," she said.

Later that week, Carli and a guest heard a loud bang that started in her closet and traveled across her floor and to her ceiling. "It was all around us," she said. "We went outside to see if someone was messing with us and every tenant in the building heard the same thing."

Later that night, Carli set up a webcam to try and capture something on video – and she did. "At 5:30 am, I caught a Shadow figure going across the screen, but it was not a shadow sticking to the walls, it was a figure passing by the camera. It appeared to be wearing a robe of some sort."

But Carli had never experienced real terror until one night she was in the apartment alone. "I was sleeping, not too deep of a sleep, when I heard a little kid walking into my room. I heard a bump and the kid crying," she said. "My first thought was it was my youngest walking in his sleep, but I did not have the kids that weekend."

Then something grabbed her bed. "The next thing you know, my whole bed was shaking violently, and I couldn't move at all," she said. "I tried to raise my head, arms, legs. Hell, I tried to get out of that room, but it was like I was being held down. I couldn't even turn my head."

Carli's bed shook for about 15 seconds, then it just stopped. "I tried to get up and still couldn't move," she said. "I tried to speak but could only get out 'wh...wh...who's ...who's th...there?' and this was a struggle to do."

Carli wants move from this apartment, but she signed a lease. "I decided to move, but for now, I am stuck in this place," she said. "But as soon as something opens up, I am getting the hell out of there."

A Feeling of Pure Evil

Pat has seen Shadow People almost all his life, but his encounters changed in middle school. "It seemed to get more frequent after that. The feeling that it left was a feeling of evil," he said. "They were pure black, I would say solid looking."

Pat saw Shadow People in his bedroom, the school library, everywhere. "It got so bad that they would just stand there watching me, and I could see them in my full vision," he said. "I was helping my mother carry in wood for our wood stove, and while my mother was in the house, I saw one clearly in daylight walking down the alley."

When the Shadow Man walked by Pat's garage, it stopped and watched him. "It stayed there staring at me," he said. "I stood there also just staring at it for awhile in shock and then went back in the house a little shaken up. I looked back outside and it was gone."

But the Shadow man wasn't gone – it never left him. "I have seen these things in various places and they seem to have been following me around everywhere," Pat said. "The feeling of pure evil is what scared the crap out of me because there were other instances in my life growing up where my mother or I also felt that strong feeling of pure evil. They have followed me most of my life."

Although Pat tries not to think about these Shadows, he truly can't stop. "I'm still curious to what exactly they are and why they are following me around."

CHAPTER 6

Red-Eyed Shadows

Shortly after her daughter was born, Liz Derringer sat in her dining room holding the newborn when something terrible came to visit. "I saw what looked like a short hooded figure with red eyes come through the wall of my dining room, stop and look at me and my daughter, then move through the basement wall," she said. "I later told my husband and he said he hadn't wanted to scare me but he'd seen it, too."

This red-eyed Shadow Person has been reported across the world. These entities are invasive and seem to feed off fear. Bishop James Long, pastor of St. Christopher Old Catholic Church in Louisville, Kentucky, has studied the paranormal for years and says these red-eyed entities are demons.

"I have found that through my research and field experience, Shadow Figures that contain red, or very dark orange color, eyes tend to be negative in nature," Long said. "The entity is clearly demonic."

Fear is what these entities are after, Long said, and will do anything to elicit fear out of their victims, including changing shape. "[They] can take the shape of many creatures," Long said. "I have seen these Shadow Entities create a figure of a black dog with red piercing eyes."

Why a black dog with glowing red eyes? They're feeding off us. "Remember, the purpose of demonic entities is to provoke fear within us," Long said. "It is that fear that it preys on, and it is that fear that it will exploit."

Kevin Dawson has felt that fear many times. "I've

met people who've seen them, and I've seen the Shadows waking and in dreams," Dawson said. "Sometimes I dream about cloaked humans. My wife still wakes up and sees them peering in the bedroom door sometimes. Whatever they are, they're rotten to the core, and thrive on negative feelings."

However, psychic Patti Starr of Lexington, Kentucky, said most encounters with red-eyed Shadow People are probably simple misidentification. On ghost investigations, Starr tries to explain a haunting with a scientific eye before considering the paranormal. "When I see things like that, I don't run. I go look at it," she said. "A lot of times I can see it was not what I thought it was. Every time I've ever had any red-eyed type experience, I've always been able to follow through and disprove it."

Shadow People, she said, are spirits, which differ from ghosts because spirits are people who've passed but occasionally come to earth to help. Ghosts are people who've died, but haven't yet passed to the other side. Although she doesn't feel the red-eyed entities are spirits, she doesn't discount the fact that they exist and terrify.

"From my own personal self, I don't know if I'd categorize [a red-eyed Shadow] as a Shadow Person," she said. "It would be a whole other category as something else." Ghosts are one explanation. Although she said seeing the apparition is rare because of the energy it takes for ghosts to manifest into something visible, it does happen. "If there was a little more distinction like a cape, a hat, red eyes, that would be a ghost taking a shape," she said. "A lot of times, ghosts having difficulty where they are will manifest into something they're part of."

But she doesn't discount the fact that these red-eyed Shadows may be something rare and evil. "I think sometimes when we see things, a lot of time if something pushes us or pinches us, we automatically think it's evil and demonic," she said. "If you're dealing with demons, it's going to hurt you. It's not going to open a door, or get up and turn the water on. Demons are serious. They're going to give you bodily harm. Evil and demonic activity, I promise you, it's not a common thing."

But why red eyes? The color red, often associated with love and seduction, has also symbolized something feared by humans across the centuries – evil. Dr. Jacqueline Kibler, professor of psychology at Northwest Missouri State University, said people may be projecting red eyes into what they determine are Shadow People because of how we're trained to think.

"Maybe we, as humans, are conditioned to believe that red is 'evil,'" she said. "Satan is often depicted as red. Blood is red, etc. Red may have more of a negative meaning, compared to other colors."

Kibler has even noted the cultural manifestation of red popping up in daily life. "On a personal note, I know some of my meditation/yoga classes have instructed us to breathe in peace – viewed as a blue color – and breathe out negativity – viewed as a red color," she said. "Maybe it is just ingrained in us."

Red, apart from being the color of blood, is also the color of fire; both of which can symbolize destruction. The Ancient Greeks associated red with their gods of war, as did Norse mythology. The planet Mars is often called the "angry red planet." Our faces become red with anger and embarrassment. And red eyes are often used to invoke terror – such as Christopher Lee's red-eyed Dracula from the 1960s/1970s vampire movies. Whatever the reason, this fear of the color red is ingrained in people worldwide.

Red-Eyed Menace

Shadow People have followed Daniel Pestana of Portugal for years. Blacker-than-night human-shaped shadows visit Daniel often – and stare. Some wear hats, some a monk's cowl. "They are never hostile to me. They seem to be mere observers," Pestana said. "I used to see them in the hallway of my house, in the reflections of mirrors and sometimes floating quickly from door to door."

He became used to these frequent visits until the night he encountered something different. Something he feels was evil. "I just saw it once," Pestana said.

He was walking his then girlfriend home when they stopped in a small park in the center of a quarter. "When we were saying good-bye to each other, we heard a noise coming from a tree [next to] a house nearby," he said. "I looked and I noticed that the top of the tree fanned itself with violence." A violent rustling and the snap of breaking branches shot through the night. "Then I heard a muffled sound of something crashing into the ground," Pestana said. "A strange feeling arose inside me that I still can't explain."

Pestana and his girlfriend watched silently as two hands grasped the top of a wall that surrounded the house's yard. "They didn't seem [like human] hands," he said. "They were dark, as if it was burned paper." As the two stood frozen, a head as dark as the hands pulled itself up from behind the wall.

"Two brilliant and red eyes stared directly at us," Pestana said. "The creature loosened a roar of some kind and it jumped upward (onto) the wall. We saw it perfectly." The figure was human-like and "pitch-black from head to toes." Neither Pestana nor his girlfriend could make out features, only the fiery red eyes.

"I grabbed my girlfriend's hand and we ran through the streets without looking back," Pestana said. "It was the only time that I felt truly threatened by those creatures."

Crazy with Fear

Becky Collins and her family moved into their new home in 2005 and almost immediately they found they were not alone.

"I have seen a Shadow Person run by me more than once," Collins said. "My son saw a black orb with smoke on it in his closet and the dog with him went crazy with fear."

But no one in her home had seen the devil her daughter saw in the dark. "My daughter woke up and there was a thing looking at her," Collins said. "It had large, red eyes with no pupil." The thing with blood-red eyes then turned and disappeared into the night.

Doors in the Collins home open and shut by themselves, and Becky blames it on the red-eyed entity – an entity that won't go away although she has had the house blessed.

Choked in the Night

Kathy Harris awakened one night unable to breathe.

"I had a horrible feeling that something was choking and crushing me," she said. "I cried out to Jesus and I opened my eyes."

A dark, hulking black shape stood beside her bed, hovering over her prone figure.

"I saw a dark Shadow with demonic red eyes next to my bed then fade away into my closet," she said. "I did not sleep for the rest of the night. I could still feel the fingers around my neck that had choked me."

Harris had seen the figure before, lurking in her backyard late at night and tapping at her bedroom door, but she'd never before felt its hands across her neck, choking her.

Now she's afraid for her life.

The Red-Eye Spoke to Me

Sleep engulfed Bobbie Morris of Rutland, Vermont, when the Shadow invaded his dreams.

"When I was 16, I was sleeping near morning," he

said. "As I was awakening, darkness overcame that dream and I looked around scared."

A Shadow creature loomed over all he saw, its red gleaming eyes burning into his. "Red Eyes told me, 'You can't leave. Bobbie. You can't leave your dream,'" he said. "It was a big booming voice, deep and frightening."

Bobbie struggled to wake, but couldn't. "I could actually feel my eyelids trying to open," he said. "It started laughing and yelled again, 'You can't escape me.'"

But somehow, Bobbie forced a scream past his lips. "I screamed myself awake," he said, waking his father, who rushed into the room. "I was wicked pale and sweat pouring. To this day I'm still confused about this."

The Dark Man

The Dark Man brought terror into the bedroom of two of Cindy Boswell's children at night. Unlike many parents, however, she believed them.

"My two younger children always talk about the 'Dark Man' or the 'Red Eyes,'" she said. "They are truly scared by these things."

Cindy never dismissed the screaming fear of her children as they seemed so sure of what they saw. "I don't ignore them and say they are just imagining them," she said. "I really listen to what they tell me. Sometimes it takes only a few minutes to calm them down – sometimes longer."

Cindy knows what her children see is real because she's seen them, too.

"For many parents, don't put the stories off that your kid tells you," she said. "Don't turn them away when they wake you up at 2 a.m. screaming in fear. Comfort them, because I for one have seen these 'Dark People' since I was small, and they can be extremely frightening."

Eyes in the Hall

The house, built in 1963 in Tampa Bay, Florida, was one of the classic Arthur Rutenberg homes that have dotted neighborhoods across Florida, Georgia, and South Carolina since 1953. And like all Rutenberg homes, it was well built and solid. Audree Tucker and her now ex-husband bought the home in the fall of 1992 and immediately noticed there was something strange about it.

The woman who'd owned the house just prior to them died, and her husband had died a few years before. "She had been a peculiar old woman, by all accounts," Tucker said. She was so peculiar, in fact, that her son wanted nothing to do with her memory. "When she died, her son sold us the house, and everything in the house, including her beautiful antiques, her clothes, her personal jewelry. We wondered why he wanted no mementos of her whatsoever."

After weeks of sorting through the woman's belongings, keeping some and selling or giving away others, the couple tried to relax in their new home, but the noises kept them awake. "The first thing we noticed after we'd moved in was the creaking at night, as if someone was tiptoeing over creaky floorboards," Tucker said. "The problem being, of course, that this was a concrete block house, and there was no wood anywhere. Certainly there was none on the floors, which were terrazzo. Okay, that was creepy, but we put it down to an old house settling."

The couple slept in the old woman's bedroom, a bedroom the woman hadn't shared with her husband. "They had that kind of old-fashioned relationship where he slept in the room down the hall, had his own bath, and she had hers," Tucker said. After the couple converted the man's bedroom into a nursery, the toilet in that bathroom started flushing continuously.

"We did what we could," Tucker said. "My husband changed the rubber thingies in the back of the toilet. He did it repeatedly, but the toilet kept flushing itself."

About the same time, the couple started hearing someone rustling the leaves outside their window at night – but when they looked, no one was there. "This was in a very good neighborhood that was well lit," she said. "There were old bushes grown up outside the windows. You could see out and in but they were formidable to get through so it wouldn't be easy for a living human to be walking directly under the windows. In fact, it wasn't possible."

But the strangeness the couple experienced around their home was limited to noise – until late one night when a six-month pregnant Audree Tucker had to use the bathroom. "One night I woke up and my bladder was calling to me," she said. "I lazily got up and went into the bathroom without closing all the doors."

While sitting on the toilet, the dark hallway open before her, she saw something that froze her to the seat. "I looked down the hallway, toward the nursery, and saw two red eyes," she said. "They were as red as Christmas tree lights and they were at the level and distance apart that eyes should be."

Thinking these lights, lights bathed in darkness, were a reflection, Tucker blinked, looked out the bathroom window to the gray sky outside, then looked back down the hall. "The eyes were still there," she said. "That's when I really started getting spooked. I knew I wasn't mistaken."

Then the eyes started to move. "The Thing started coming down the hall toward me," Tucker said. "I screamed like only Jamie Lee Curtis [in the movie *Halloween*] can scream and my husband woke up and turned on the light in a flash, and The Thing was gone."

Tucker's husband searched the house, but found no trace of an intruder. The windows were sealed, the doors were locked. "After that I decided it was time to do something. I settled on praying The Thing out of my house," she said. "I prayed all the time. By the time the baby was born, the noises had gone and I never saw The Thing again. But what was it?"

An Encounter After Surgery

Dawn Sevier of Sparta, Tennessee, has experienced Shadow People often, but none as terrifying as the thing she encountered while recovering from surgery. "I had just been released from the hospital, and was heavily medicated," she said. "I'd had a bad experience in the hospital; suddenly I couldn't tolerate morphine and it arrested my breathing. I had one of those experiences where you disconnect from your body and watch everything that's going on."

Dawn was staying with a friend because she couldn't be alone. During the first night at her friend's house, she saw herself leave her body. "I was sleeping and I found myself standing next to myself, watching myself sleep," she said. "As I stood there, I could sense that someone was standing to my left – behind me – but I couldn't turn and look, I was blocked from turning. I could look to my right, and when I did, the wall began vibrating faster and faster."

Suddenly a Shadow Person walked through the wall. "It was uncloaked and its appearance was like looking at black oil," Dawn said. "Its body was muscular, its head was large, no hair, and its eyes were black and red."

Dawn stood next to her body and watched the creature. The entity had almond-shaped eyes, a small nose and small mouth set in an oval-shaped head. But the main feature was its veins. "It had red blood veins, like humans have blue ones, running all over it's muscular structure," she said. "It stood about seven feet tall, and it couldn't see me at all."

She stood, staring at the creature when she realized it was looking at something specific – it was looking at her body. "I noticed that it was looking at me laying in bed," she said. "I suddenly felt like fighting and looked down at its feet, only it had no feet. Its legs faded to black-and-red mist, and as I saw this I had an urge to jump into my body that was sleeping."

As this urge swept through her, the human qualities of the Shadow Man dissipated into a cloud of black and red mist. The mist rose above her body forming a column, and began wrapping itself around her feet and ankles, snaking its way up the length of her body.

"Suddenly, I found myself throwing covers off myself and screaming, 'no,'" Dawn said. "I demanded that the thing leave me alone, I told it that it couldn't touch me."

As Dawn sat in bed – now awake – draped in an icy cold, sheets and nightgown soaked with sweat, she was not afraid. She was curious and angry, but not afraid. "I felt anger at its attempt to invade my space," she said.

The Shadow in the Hall

A Shadow stalked a hallway in the apartment where Garrett spent most of his childhood. "At first I was terrified but eventually I got used to him," Garrett said. "He had really negative energy."

One night, as young Garrett tried to sleep, he saw the Shadow Man in his closet. "It was pitch black in my room but he was darker than that," Garrett said. "He had red eyes [and] he was terrifying. I hid under the covers and prayed until I fell asleep and I never saw him again."

But Garrett has seen other Shadows. "Often I see them when I walk down the street and usually I am very afraid."

CHAPTER 7

Buzzing Shadows

As a teen, Frank Byner was tormented by Shadow People. Two to three times a week, Byner would wake to find a Shadow Person standing by his bed, a dark silhouette against the gray walls of night. But Byner's visitations and their effects – his clenched chest, his panicked breath – were different from any Shadow Person experience covered so far.

His Shadow People were buzzing. "I remember experiencing the sensation of loud buzzing going through my body," Byner said. "It felt kind of like electricity." As Byner lie in bed, the Shadow Man looming at his bedside, the buzzing rattled his entire body. "It felt like someone was poking me with something electric," he said. "There was an entity in the house I lived in at the time that made itself known."

Although reports of this buzzing sound during Shadow People encounters are rare, Dr. Dave Oester of the International Ghost Hunters Society and an 18-year ghost-hunting veteran said this buzzing is often heard during encounters with ghosts, which is what he feels Shadow People are. "The sound of buzzing or chirping is a common phenomenon with ghosts," he said. "It is caused by the rapid movement in the air causing the air to vibrate."

Ghosts, he said, have mass and density so they cast shadows and can affect the local air pressure. "It takes more energy to manifest noise, but so what? They have the energy to do it. Why limit them?" Oester said. "I have personally heard them speak, chat." He's heard their footsteps, their closing doors, "as well as turning on electrical devices, removing physical objects and moving them to other locations."

Fellow ghost hunter Alexandra Gargiulo said this buzzing sound isn't just reserved for Shadow People and ghosts. "Angels are said, as I have actually witnessed myself, [to have] a buzzing noise as if they really do have wings fluttering at high rates of speed creating a buzzing effect," she said. "They're not all white and do come in all sizes, shapes, and colors."

But do they come as Shadows?

High-Pitched Whine

Twelve-year-old Carl Phillips awoke around 3:30 a.m., his bedroom gray and unfriendly. Fear took him when he realized he was paralyzed. "I couldn't move my arms or me head," Phillips said. "I could still see and hear though."

A Shadow Man stood near a cabinet in the corner of his room – watching him. As Phillip laid there in terror, a strange buzzing noise filled the room. "I remember a high-pitched whine," he said. "And this horrible, horrible sense of dread."

Phillips fought to move, but couldn't. He soon gave up and darkness gripped him. "I blacked out, and when I opened my eyes, I screamed out loud and ran out of my room into my mom's room," he said.

Since that night, Phillips often sees these mysterious, walking Shadows. "I haven't had any experiences as bad as that since, but I have seen those Shadow People," Phillips said. "My heart skips a beat and I either run up to a real person to stand by for the feeling of safety, or I run away as fast as I can."

The Sound of Bees

It was in the early hours of a day in 1974 in Laguna Beach, California, when Grover Bonham realized someone was in his house.

"I was in the Army from 1966 to 1968," Bonham said. "I have traveled around this dirt-ball alone for more years than I care to remember. I grew up on the streets of L.A., and little causes me to feel fear." But until then he'd never encountered the paranormal.

"I woke up and could not move anything but my eyes," he said. "There was an 'energy' blanket covering me and it scared the shit out of me."

Then he saw the intruders. Two black human figures, about four-feet tall and thin, stood about three to four feet from his bed. He couldn't make out their faces but they frightened him. "They made no threatening moves or gestures," Bonham said. "They were not doing anything to cause me to be so terrified."

Then Bonham noticed a noise, a noise that shouldn't have been in his house. "They were making a sound that sounded like the buzzing of bees," he said. Bonham tried to scream, but the sound died in his throat when he realized these entities were communicating with him. "A voice came into my head and said that if I needed to be free of the energy that was holding me down I should start with a low hum and as the energy starts to dissipate, make it louder until I feel safe," he said. "That is what I did and [to] the point where I could move my hand."

As Bonham began to move, the two Shadow People walked through a slit in the air and were gone. At that point I could move freely," he said. "I told no one, not even my Yoga-Master."

But the Shadow People weren't finished with Bonham – they returned three years later. "I was in bed sleeping with my then girlfriend Chadwick," Bonham said. "I woke up with that same feeling of not being able to move.

There were three of them in my room, two at the side of my bed and one sitting on my legs. I freaked."

He tried to call his girlfriend but no words would come. Bohnam relaxed and followed the advice given him during his first encounter. "I started to hum," he said. "When I did that, the one on my legs stood up on my bed and knocked a corner of a tapestry loose that was hanging over my bed. All three went through the slit and I had free movement."

Just as in his first encounter, he couldn't make out features on their faces. They were just black. "It was like a haze engulfed the room while they were there," he said. "It was no dream."

This encounter repeated itself the next year. "I was in bed with my then girlfriend Susie and woke up with that same feeling of not being able to move," he said. "Again, it scared the shit out of me."

The three Shadow People were back, standing near his bed, just watching. "I had no reason for the level of fear I felt," Bonham said. "They made no move to harm myself or Susie and were again talking and it sounded like bees buzzing."

Again he couldn't talk, and again he began to hum. "The louder I got, the more the energy dissipated, and the three beings again walked through a slit in the air," he said.

He then shook Susie awake and told her all of his Shadow People encounters. She didn't believe him – until five years later. "Susie and I parted ways a year later but stayed good friends," he said. "In 1983, I received a phone call from Susie. She was excited and would not say why over the phone."

She asked him to come to the house where she was taking care of five-year-old twins, Robin and Rachael, while their parents were in Tibet. "After I walked into the house, Susie told Robin and Rachael, 'tell Grover what happened last night,'" he said.

What the girls told him flooded him with memories of his encounters. "The girls told me a story of how four Shadow People came to their room and visited with them the night before," he said. "They sounded like bees buzzing when they talked and [they were] nice."

The Shadow beings visited the girls for about 20 minutes. Neither girl had been paralyzed like Bonham and neither experienced Bonham's energy blanket. "I asked if they were afraid, they laughed and said no, why would they be?" he said. "Even though Robin and Rachael could not understand the buzzing, they could hear the being's thoughts. It was no big thing to Robin and Rachael and they laughed at my obvious fear."

They also knew why Bonham had been pinned down and they had not. "They said I had to be 'kept safe' so I would not try to hurt the Shadow People or myself," Bonham said. "I felt like a wimp. These two five-year-old girls had no fear at all. Why should they? The Shadow People meant no harm."

The Shadow People told the girls they were here as observers from a parallel dimension, nothing more, nothing less. "They have, to date, not returned to me," Bonham said. "I am truly sorry that I did not have it together enough to be cool. [But] I had never in my life felt fear like I did during my first contact with these beings."

Vibrations in My Head

Jenny Mayes gets jittery when she hears about Shadow People.

"Anytime I read a book or read about someone's personal experience and it matches one of mine exactly, I get this shot of, I guess, panic through me," she said. "I think maybe because it confirms what I have seen and been through is real."

As in Bonham's encounters, Jenny has awoken paralyzed by Shadow People, a buzzing noise filling her bedroom. "It's an intense buzzing/vibration in my head that fades fairly quickly after becoming conscious," she said. "The paralysis wears off about the time the buzzing goes away."

But Jenny doesn't attribute her experiences to a Shadow Person that's ghostly or inter-dimensional. "It's abductions," she said. "Alien abduction experiences. I call them aliens because that's what makes the most sense to me...They're not human, and presumably not from this earth, and seem to be interested in doing experiments on people."

Her last experience was 12 years ago. "Terrifying is an understatement," she said. "There is not a word in the English language that can adequately describe the terror and fear of these experiences. I just hope they are done with me. I will do anything possible and use any means necessary to kill them, stop them, or persuade them that I'm not worth it. And I am going to be as hostile and violent as possible."

CHAPTER 8

Angry, Hooded Shadows

A black, cloaked, man-like figure stood in thirteen-year-old David's room, staring at him. "I see these things a lot," David said. "They scare me so much." David can do nothing but watch as the entity looms over him.

David thinks it's feeding. "I read that sometimes when people are afraid of the unknown, dark entities are attracted to them and they feed off their fear. I don't know what these Dark Hooded Figures are. I've never seen their face and they are always standing at my doorway. They disappear as quickly as they came. Can't anyone tell me what they are?"

Psychic Dawn Newlan of the Ozark Paranormal Society has seen entities like this and knows how frightening they can be. It's "an evil entity," Newlan said. "The fear it sends through your body is something hard to describe, but you know with every inch of your existence that what you are in the presence of is not good and you should not be there."

Reports of cloaked Shadow People are worldwide. Why would people from the United States, Sweden, South Africa, and Australia see the same entity?

Parapsychologist Loyd Auerbach said it's probably societal. "Besides the Shadow People, there are reported sightings of the Grim Reaper," he said. "It's likely there's a psychological component in many of these sightings."

That's what worries Lindsie Harlan of Austin, Texas – that she's seeing the Grim Reaper. Lindsie often wrestles with sleep. One night in the spring of her senior year in high school, the math education major at Austin Community College awoke to find something dark and cloaked in shadows.

"I was asleep and I just woke up for no reason and there was this huge tall black figure standing on the side of my bed," Lindsie said. "Its legs were all the way to the ceiling and it was staring down at me with two beady, shiny eyes."

Lindsie lay in bed, the hooded figure staring down at her. "I didn't move because I was afraid if I moved it would know I was alive and try to kill me," she said. "I felt as if I was paralyzed from the eyes down." As many people experiencing ghosts and Shadow Beings have reported, Lindsie was able to shut her eyes and, strangely, fall back to sleep.

She didn't talk to anyone about the experience until her second paranormal encounter later that summer, then she told her mother. "She got scared for me," Lindsie said. "She started going into this whole thing about Jesus and to say 'in the name of Jesus, I command you to go away.' She also said something about 'death comes knocking on peoples door all the time, you just have to be careful.' Do you really think it's death?"

The tall, black, hooded Shadow hasn't visited Lindsie in the night since, but that doesn't leave her comforted. She's still waiting for the night something cloaked in shadows glares at her in the darkness. "I find it hard to go to sleep," she said. "I am so paranoid that the next time I open my eyes I'm going to see something else that will scare me."

The Shadow Highway

Luci and her husband were moving from Oregon to Ohio in 2003 when they encountered something they never expected. "We were severely sleep deprived, and on the evening of day two I began to notice something very odd," Luci said. "I was seeing amorphous, floating, black, cloaked and hooded figures skimming about six inches to a foot off the ground."

Some of the beings were standing still, but most seemed to be "heading somewhere definite," Luci said, and traveling as fast as the moving truck her husband drove. "I saw them here and there every few minutes, and I couldn't help but feel disturbed," she said. "Though I was quite tired, I felt wide awake and everything else I saw looked completely normal."

As they drove east, the sightings continued, almost like Luci was catching a glimpse of another highway in another realm. "I was amazed every time I saw another Shadow figure," she said. "Several passed over the highway crossing our path as we drove. For the few hours when this happened, I saw them through dusk, dark, and into the next morning."

Luci and her husband stopped for a rest that morning after an encounter that got too close. "Towards dawn one Shadow figure passed right through the cab of our moving truck," Luci said. "I clearly saw the drape of the folds of the encompassing cloak, though the face and head were hidden deep in a cowl. I couldn't help but gasp and pull away, too stunned to worry about how crazy my actions might seem to my husband."

But he noticed her jump, and Luci was surprised that he knew why. "He turned and looked at me and said, 'You saw it too?'" she said. "I was astonished. But at last we were able to compare notes, and it seemed we were seeing the same thing. What's more, we were seeing the exact same figures at the exact same time."

They began pointing out the cloaked, hooded Shadow People as they drove, slightly relieved they weren't going crazy. "Neither of us had been ingesting any substances or drinking anything but coffee, so these mutual 'hallucinations' were perplexing," Luci said. "All we could guess was that the lull of the truck engine over hundreds of miles and both of us being sleep deprived made it easier to see beings that were perhaps of the astral plane."

That's when they began to get nervous. "When two people start seeing figures of death seemingly everywhere, they might worry for their longevity all of a sudden," she said. "We pulled off to stop at a motel shortly after we admitted to one another that we were seeing these things."

The couple arrived in Ohio safely and has lived there since – but their drive through the astral plane seemed to open a door they can't shut. "Since then, my husband and I have both seen these beings a couple of times a year, usually just 'passing through' our yard or house," Luci said. "They ignore us for the most part, though once I chased one down and put my hands right through it."

When Luci's hands sank into the chest of the Shadow Person, she felt an "odd, chilled, deep vibration" crawl through her. "The Shadow Person stopped when I did this, and I got the distinct impression that his kind are not used to being seen, let alone chased down and poked," Luci said. "But, apparently, they can see us well enough, and 'feel' us, too."

The Finger

Debbie saw an angry, hooded Shadow when she was 12 years old, and worse yet, it saw her. "My mother has drug-induced schizophrenia and would get really weird and crazy," Debbie said. "One night we were fighting really bad, and I told her that she wasn't my mother and that I wanted my mother back. She kept on telling me that she was my mother and I kept on telling her I wanted my mother back and that she was possessed by evil."

After the argument, Debbie went to bed – but something was waiting for her. "This black Shadow appeared in the corner of the room," Debbie said. "It slowly came forward and got bigger as it approached me, it looked hooded and black." The creature "flipped me off and had a very long middle finger."

The vision quickly faded away and young Debbie dismissed it as a hallucination, until her half-sister admitted she had also seen the entity. "She said she saw this same thing in a graveyard and that six of her friends saw it too," Debbie said. "She said she was really intrigued by it and it had glowing red eyes."

The Shadow Man Invades

When she was 15, Dawn Sevier was walking across a Jacksonville Beach, Florida, apartment parking lot when she had her first encounter with a Shadow. "I was getting into [my friend's] car and I caught sight of the Shadow entity," Sevier said. "It was cloaked, and there were eyes of fire inside the hood of the cloak. I stared at it, and it stared back at me. I wasn't frightened."

She turned and asked her friend if she saw the hooded Shadow Man, too. "She thought I was nuts," Sevier said. "She couldn't see it, but I could. It hovered at least six feet off the ground and watched us as we left the parking lot."

She didn't see the entity again until she was 24 and lived in Tennessee. "It was day time, in the morning hours, and I was attending a church service," she said. "I couldn't see any eyes this time, and this Shadow Person moved about among the people there. If anyone else could see it, they didn't make it known."

But that wasn't the last time she saw the Shadow Man in church. Months later she sat in the same church when a Shadow Person walked up to the speaker and stepped inside him. "The shape of the person's face became distorted, as if it was being bent across a pole, the forehead leaning to the right, the nose to the left, and the lower portion of the face again was bent to the right side," she said. "The eyes of the speaker changed to black – a deep,

deep black, and this thing looked at me."

Fear flushed through her and she began looking to see if anyone else had seen this when reality changed. "I noticed that everyone was moving in slow motion," she said. "I also noticed that sounds had slowed down, as if a tape recorder were running very slowly. I realized at that moment that these Shadows must be resonating at a higher rate of speed than we are, and this is why they are undetectable to most people."

Dawn believes that somehow she had tuned into the frequency where Shadow People operate. "I could see as well as hear and feel the atmosphere that surrounds a Shadow Person," she said. "The stare of this thing was beyond any fright I've ever known," she said. "And I'm still not sure if it was my fright I was feeling, or that of the Shadow entity. All I can say is that I felt deep fear."

After about ten minutes, the entity stepped out of the man and disappeared. "The man stumbled back a little, and said he felt dizzy," Dawn said. "He had no idea something had entered his body and then left it."

A Growing Anger

Joseph was 18 when he moved into his first apartment, but he didn't stay long as the apartment was angry. "There was tension in the apartment," Joseph said. "The longer I lived there, the stronger the tension would get. As I would walk across the rooms, I would feel sensations going through me."

Joseph felt the anger growing in his apartment, but that didn't prepare him for what followed. "One night I woke up and looked at the foot of my bed," Joseph said. "There was a blacker-than-night creature. It spun around like it was angry and confused. I felt the whole presence of it at the foot of my bed."

He turned on the light and the thing was gone. Then two weeks later, it returned. "I was visited [by] one that was about seven-foot tall with a hood and a cape," Joseph said. "It just came up to my side of the bed and towered over me. I felt such fear I was paralyzed. It just stood there like it was looking through me. I covered my head like a kid. This one was bold and meant to bring about fear, and I knew it." When Joseph grew brave enough to peel off the blanket, the figure was gone, but the fear remained.

After that night, Joseph rarely stayed in his apartment alone, but anyone staying there also saw the entity. "My brother saw them," he said. "A friend of mine woke me up screaming one night. She had seen one of them, so I knew it wasn't only me."

Joseph eventually moved. "I am just glad they didn't follow me," he said.

Joseph's experience isn't unique.

"My brother-in-law saw one of these things in his apartment. It was not friendly – at all," Bill from St. Louis said. "He said he could feel the anger directed toward him. He saw it. Tall, dark, no face, with a hood."

Was It a Dream?

The boys shared a bedroom growing up and changed the position of the furniture often, just to keep things new. But when the brothers moved James' bed in front of the door, his nights changed, James said, speaking of where in the room he and his brother would bed down. "There was one time where my bed was logically placed about three feet away from and adjacent to the bedroom door. I would have rather normal nights of sleep; nothing overly unusual. However, I would start to get this reoccurring dream."

In the dream, James was asleep, facing a wide-open door opening into a hallway and the bottom three stairs of a stairway that went to the second floor. "I would see a hooded figure like a monk come down the stairs, which descended the same direction that I was laying," he said.

"This figure would always do the same thing: it would descend the staircase, pause a moment near the last step to look over to where I was laying – and then the whole episode would just kind of go away."

James is now an adult and isn't so sure those encounters were just dreams. "I was sleeping – I thought – during all of these instances," he said. "This figure would not have a face, and seemed to be very human-like and not skeletal. I could see the hood turning as if it were noticing my presence, though I do not know for sure that it was looking over at me as it simply could have been looking in my direction."

The dreams were identical – the creature would descend the stairs, stare at James, and disappear. "I have no idea how any of them end as I have no memory past the point where it looked at me," he said. "I never woke with fear, as it was almost as if I was watching a movie rather than experiencing it myself. It was always unnerving."

But James only had the dream when he slept in front of the door. "It only happened when my bed was placed in such a way that I had a clear visual out through the bedroom door," he said. James no longer lives in that house, and has not dreamed the dream of the hooded Shadow Man since he moved.

Attacking the Terror

A woman with the online name Truthseeker has also seen the hooded figure. "I was laying in bed at night, unable to sleep, [when] a dark black figure floated about a foot or two above my bed," she said. "His head looked like it was hooded, no detail other than that. It was very menacing and obviously not a good thing."

The visits soon became frequent and Truthseeker had had enough of them. "I sat up in the bed and I actually took a swing at this thing," she said. "The instant my fist would have come in contact with it, it vanished. I was shocked, although I'm not sure what I was expecting. I just let my anger and frustration come out."

It must have worked, as the black, hooded figure hasn't visited Truthseeker since. "I felt very good after I figured out that I had 'defeated' it that night," she said.

But Mikk, an eBay salesman from Toronto, has seen the angry, hooded Shadow, and fought it almost to his death. Mikk lived, but he fears for others.

The Angel of Death

A streetlight glowed through a second-story window in North York, Toronto, bathing a bedroom in dull yellow light. Mikk, 17, was sleeping in that bedroom in 1977 the night he met an entity he can only describe as Death. "Deep in sleep I was woken by a sharp kick to the ribs," Mikk said. "My ribs hurt for weeks."

Mikk gasped for air, but he couldn't call for help, he couldn't breathe. "I thought there was someone in my closet who'd hit me with a hockey stick and went back into the closet," he said. But, as he lie gasping in his bed, he could only stare as the corners of his room bent toward him, as though reality had changed.

Then a gurgling noise erupted. "I think, 'what the heck is this now?'" he said. "It's coming from my stomach for some reason. I try to yell for help and I can't utter a peep."

Trapped, breathless, alone, Mikk laid on his bed, moving his head and trying to see the closet door. He still thought someone was in there – he was almost right. "I'm keeping my eye on the closet door not knowing if there's someone in there or not," he said. "But no sooner had I focused on that, there was what I can only describe as a psychic explosion."

Heavy smoke blew into Mikk's room then drew together into a human shape – a shape Mikk will never forget. "A hooded monk-like entity with no legs," he said.

"It barks at me 'questions, questions,' right off the top. It wanted me to realize it was there, and I thought 'whoa.'"

The entity loomed over Mikk, prodding him with the repeated phrase, "questions, questions." "I'm just a kid," Mikk said. "I don't have any clever questions. I should have asked for lotto numbers."

Then the entity turned and its profile became as two-dimensional as a pencil mark. Mikk thought, "if Dad catches you, it's toast," and the entity turned from its two-dimensional line and faced him. "No one's going to help you," it said.

Suddenly the entity pointed at Mikk, its arms skeletal. The pointing finger extended across the room and hit Mikk's face. "Then, boom, it's absolute darkness now," Mikk said. "This entity is so evil, light avoids it."

Mikk demanded the entity leave, but to no effect. Then the struggle moved into Mikk's psyche. "Suddenly a door appears in my mind. I step through this door and now I'm inside my mind. It's very much akin to a large hotel complex," Mikk said. "I'm loath to open the doors, but I do and there's these colorful Easter eggs that have pictures of my old memories. Suddenly my mind takes over and I start whipping through these hallways."

As Mikk's memories rush through his mind, he senses the entity feeding off his hate, his lust, his fears. "Distilled male hatred and avarice," Mikk said. "It was not so much evil as pure unadulterated sin – and it's not ashamed of it."

Then Mikk felt himself weakening. "I realize this is killing me," he said. "It's taking away my memories that are very much a part of me. I look for a grip somewhere and suddenly a meter appears, of all things. Very much like a VU meter on a recorder."

Mikk said this vision was his mind's representation of the life draining from his body – and the meter was going down. "When it finally stopped doing this memory download, he's bending over me listening to my stomach gurgles." The gurgles, Mikk figured, were the sounds of his soul. The entity wanted that, too.

Then the thing leapt on top of Mikk and pushed his soul through the mattress. "This is the mother of all ghosts," Mikk said. "It just squashed me and I was hanging on for dear life. I was youthful and full of life."

Mikk then left his body and traveled to the other side. The entity invited him to stay, but Mikk said 'no,' and, for a reason Mikk still doesn't understand, the thing released him. "I just thought 'I want to be home.' And as soon as I thought this, I fell," he said. "I came crashing down into my body. And I woke up a few minutes later and, glory be, it wasn't here. Then I slept through the night. I woke up and sunshine never looked so great."

Mikk thought his experience was over, but in 1999, a newspaper description of the "Bedroom Rapist" in the Scarborough neighborhood of Toronto, made him realize his attacker might still be terrorizing people. "I was just happy to have survived the whole deal," Mikk said. "And it wasn't until I read that story in *The Toronto Star,* 'Woman confronts pure evil,' that I realized there's this dark Shadowy entity that's bothering people in their sleep."

The memory of Mikk's encounter engulfed him again. He poured through newspapers, looking for more accounts of the "dark Shadowy entity" and found that description had been used numerous times to describe the "Bedroom Rapist."

He also noticed that description had been used to describe a figure associated with cat mutilations around the city. "I contact the police and they said they are aware of the paranormal aspect," Mikk said. "They told me not to speak to anybody about it." But he knows we need to be aware. "These entities are sinister and powerful and don't hesitate to use it," he said. "When your shields are down, it's when they get their foot in the door."

And once they're in, you're in danger.

CHAPTER 9

Shadows that Attack

Many people who encounter Shadow People are convinced the entities are demons, negative entities who feed off fear. Although paranormal investigator Alexandra Gargiulo – daughter of famous ghost hunter Hanz Holzer – is certain of the existence of demons, she's not ready to slap the label "demon" onto Shadow People. "This is hard because it is one of those situations that needs to be documented a lot before any real belief is formed on the topic," she said. "We need to have more evidence on this. But, if one would take a gander at its presence, it would obviously be evil and in the demonic range." Although not physical beings themselves, demons – quite possibly the fallen angels of the Bible – can and do assist a human who is out to harm. "Negative energy and souls who behave badly will attract these more than anyone else," Gargiulo said.

Exorcist James Bucknam of Beverly, Massachusetts, is convinced Shadow People are an ancient evil. Although Bucknam has successfully removed ghosts, poltergeists, Shadow People, and the occasional demon from homes for the past 13 years, he cautions people who try to interact with them. "Shadow People can be one of the most difficult entities to get rid of because they tend to be very tenacious once they decide to visit a person on a regular basis." And these entities are never alone – Bucknam said they always operate in groups. "They are negative in their orientation," he said. "And must be dealt with carefully." Bucknam's best piece of advice is to avoid any activity that might invite a Shadow Man into your life. "Exposing yourself to them could lead to disruptions in your life of a negative variety."

Many people have reported being attacked by Shadow People. Most are like Francisco from Toronto, who was dragged from sleep by dark, heavy hands in February 2005. "I went to sleep around 1 o'clock after a long chat with [my sister]," Francisco said. "I had nothing to drink, I didn't do any drugs, and I was very aware of what happened."

As Francisco slept, a buzzing noise crept into his sleep, getting louder and louder. "All of the sudden the buzzing noise got closer and I wake up in my bed choking," Francisco said. "When I open my eyes I see a black Shadow on top of my body choking me."

Francisco fought with the Shadow, trying to push away the gripping hands, but he couldn't touch his Shadow attacker. "I rolled out of the bed and fell on the floor, but the entity was still choking me," he said. "I tried to call my sister but she couldn't [hear] my call. I saw her moving in bed, but she never woke up."

As Francisco wheezed for breath, the entity suddenly released him. "It stared at me from the corner of the room," he said, "until it disappeared." Later that week, Francisco learned that his best friend had committed suicide the night the Shadow man attacked. "I was so scared, I didn't know what to think," he said. "I never had an explanation for it."

Violated by a Shadow Man

Anne Williams of Sydney, Australia, was roused at 3 a.m. one day in 2005 by something in her room. It was not friendly. "One early morning I felt so strongly that there was a presence standing next to my left as my bed was right in the corner of the wall," Anne said. "I felt as though I was blocked, like something was standing over me or wanted to scare me."

She didn't understand what she saw. "As I opened my eyes to see what the hell it was, there stood on my left side of the bed a black cloaked hooded figure," she said. The thing leaned over Anne, its face gray and snowy "like a TV screen when it's all fuzzy," Ann said. Its eyes were black and sunken in the snowy face. "I screamed and instantly I was pinned to the bed, the only body part I could move was my neck area, everything else was locked to the bed," she said.

Anne lay on her back, trying to scream as the figure leaned into her. "I felt that it shoved its arm down my neck and was choking me, as nothing came out of my mouth," she said. "Like no noise. I could not even hear myself scream, but I was."

Tears ran down her face, soaking her pillow as she tried to scream but couldn't. "I was trying to get up, which I could not," she said. "I felt that it was trying to scare me to death."

Then the cloaked figure's attack grew worse. "After a while all of these horrible things are happening, I got more strength in myself," she said. "The figure decided to scare me more. It half went inside me and was cold like ice. As it went in me I felt so sick."

That's when Anne got angry. "I started to get pissed off as this piece of shit was trying to hurt me," she said. "So I thought, that's it I'm going to pray to God."

She lay there, still pinned to the bed, choking, crying and trying to scream. "I really felt that I was going to have a heart attack as this thing was so powerful," she said. "I had the strength in my soul to pray to God and ask for it to leave me alone."

Then she opened her eyes to look into the snowy, cloaked face of her attacker. "I said angrily in my soul, "leave me alone, whatever you are. Leave me alone, you are not welcome to be in my body,'" Anne said. "It's mine. You don't belong here."

Finally, the cloaked Shadow Man let her go. "I got up all in a sweat and I was like, 'I saw a ghost.' I felt victimized, and felt like no one could help me," she said. "Well, I know that God helped me."

Anne still doesn't understand exactly what happened. Her mother told her it was the spirit of a rapist. "I don't know what it was, but I feel that it was evil and wanted to kill me," Anne said. "I wonder why this happened to me? It's all a mystery."

The Shadow being returned the next day, but Anne said prayer drove the black, cloaked thing from her. "I flew out of bed and prayed to God to take it away," she said. "I opened my eyes and it was gone. Thank God for His help."

But the thing wasn't gone forever. A year later, Anne was living in another house when the Shadow came back. "Again, it was early in the morning," she said. "I was sleeping on my right side, and in my ear someone whispered in a male voice, 'I'm here.' I was so tired, I just said in a mumble, 'Go away, I want to sleep.' I felt a chill when it was next to me, and I felt sick when it spoke to me."

Anne doesn't know if her attacker was a demon, or a ghost, but she hasn't been visited again.

Beaten by a Shadow

When Cathy Moreno of O'Fallon, Illinois, fell asleep early one Friday night in December 2007, she didn't expect to wake up and find a monster. "I woke up a little after 3 a.m. and I couldn't go back to sleep, so I watched some TV," Cathy said. "Out of nowhere I suddenly got a headache and felt sick to my stomach. Needless to say I ended up getting sick. At that point, I didn't want the TV on, I just wanted to lay back down."

But as Cathy was dozing, around 5 a.m. she heard a low-level frequency sound in her left ear, followed by a whisper. "It was a loud whisper, which sounded almost like a different language," she said. "I opened my eyes to see this Shadow figure hovering over me."

As soon as she saw it, the Shadow began slamming into her. "Every time it hit, it was like a ringing sound in my ears," she said. "My body went into some kind of convulsion – which really freaked me out, but it only lasted a few seconds."

She tried to scream, but no sound came out. "I mean, I tried hard to scream," she said. "But it was like it took my voice. I finally just said, 'leave me alone,' even though there was no sound coming out."

The attack ended just as quickly as it had begun, and Cathy could speak again. "I tested out my voice and sure enough, it was back," she said.

One thing about the Shadow attacker stood out for Cathy – unlike most descriptions of Shadow People, this Shadow was a woman. "I felt like this entity was a female," she said. "The voice I heard was a female, but the Shadow was very androgynistic, like it didn't have a sex to it."

Cathy has since tried to find an explanation for her attack. "I've never had any kind of paranormal experience before," she said. "I can't say that I didn't believe it, but just never really thought I'd ever experience anything like this, let alone of this magnitude."

One possible explanation for her experiences is sleep paralysis, but Cathy quickly dismissed this possibility. "I know that sleep paralysis is something that many people would think happened," she said. "All I can say to those is, unless you have actually been attacked in this way, I wouldn't chalk other people's experience up to that. Having experienced this, I know that I was attacked by something."

These Shadow entities, Cathy believes, feed off fear. That's one possible reason her attack ended so soon after it began. "From the moment I was attacked, I don't believe there was any moment that I was really scared," she said. "I was more shocked and remember thinking, 'what the hell is happening?' But I'm not a fearful person in general. I can definitely see how fear can create an energy for these things to feed off."

To keep her attacker at bay, Cathy has taken to lighting a white unscented candle and saying Psalm 91 – "He that dwelleth in the secret place of the Most High shall abide under the Shadow of the Almighty" – before sleep. "You just never know," she said.

Attack in England

Alisha Bernadette Gillam of London began seeing Shadow People in her home, nestled in a block of apartment buildings, when she was 10 years old. "It petrifies me to think about it," she said. "My parents' bedroom seemed to be the heart of where the Shadow Being used to come from."

Gillam's mother would send her upstairs to fetch a coffee cup she often left on her bedside table – and that's where she first saw him. "I would walk in and go towards the cup, then I would see this huge dark Shadow, a male being in a big black cape with a hood," Gillam said. "It was like a massive moving silhouette. It had spikes coming from its back and claws coming from the sleeve of his cape. I knew it was male, I knew it was evil."

Frightened, Gillam couldn't move. "I wanted to run, but I couldn't. I wanted to scream, but I couldn't," she said. "I tried to scream, and I thought I was screaming, but it was like someone picked up a remote and put me on mute." She stood, frozen, tears streaming down her face, as the Shadow Man approached.

"The Shadow would circle the room, then it would glide slowly towards me," she said. "All I could hear was, 'ba-boom, ba-boom, ba-boom.' It was so loud it was like a heartbeat put on high volume."

Gillam dropped to the floor and curled into a ball.

"I put my hands over my ears and closed my eyes tight shut, but every time I opened them it was still gliding towards me," she said.

The thing stopped right next to her, then disappeared. "It was like I was released," she said. "It felt like someone had just let go of me. My movement came back and I shot out the door, came running down the stairs and be in hysterics telling my mum ... she never believed me."

Over the next few years, Gillam's encounters grew steadily worse. "If I even walked past the room – not enter it, but walk past – it would drag me in, my whole body was being pulled by this strong force in to the bedroom. I would scream and cry and try and run the opposite direction, but it was too strong."

Pulled into her mother's bedroom, Gillam would drop into the fetal position and pray for the Shadow Man to go away. "Sometimes I knew it was coming as I would hear the heartbeat," she said. "Then my body would freeze."

The attacks often occurred when her family was downstairs in the living room. They never knew what was happening. "One time I needed the bathroom and as I was about to walk past my mum and dad's bedroom to get there, it started dragging me into the room," Gillam said. "I grabbed hold of the banister and pulled with all my might to stay where I was then. Next thing I know both my legs are being lifted off the ground. It was pulling me into my parents' bedroom. I was screaming, crying, everything and no one downstairs could hear me."

Somehow, Gillam hooked her legs around the banister and the thing could pull her no further. "I tried to run down the steps," she said. "The first three or four steps was like going down in slow motion there was a force pushing me back, then it was like I was released. I went flying forwards and spun at the bottom of the stairs and ran straight to my parents to tell them...they did not believe me."

At age twelve, Gillam's family started attending church regularly and her mother enrolled her in a Church of England School and the attacks stopped. Gillam is now 22 years old, married, and living in a different apartment. Only once when she was 19 has she felt the Shadow Person there. "One night I was on my own in the flat and I felt its presence," she said. "I could hear the heartbeat; it was faint this time, but I never saw the Shadow. I just stared at the door waiting for it to come in the room. It never did."

Now that the Shadow Man has drifted into her past, all she wants are answers. "What is it?" she asked. "Where did it come from? Was it a demon? Why did it look so scary? Why me? The weirdest thing about it is, although I don't see it anymore, deep down – although it scares the shit out of me and I don't want it to come back – there's something inside me that wants to see it again."

The Thing Dropped Me

One night when Terri was in junior high school, she was awakened by an electric charge that left a tingling cold throughout her body. "It was like a low-level vibration," Terri said.

Terri scanned the room, but her glasses were sitting on her nightstand and she couldn't make out more than shadowy blobs in the room. "I couldn't clearly see anything, but did feel like I was being watched," she said. "I am certain there was a Shadow Person in the room with me that night.

"I have had falling dreams that were more than dreams. I would wake up after feeling myself being dropped from ceiling height. I would slam hard into the bed and get the wind knocked out of me often. I think I was being lifted by something and then when I started to wake up, it dropped me and hid."

Terri said the couple that sold her parents the house

was paranoid about something there. "For years we didn't experience anything until the events I mentioned," she said. "I haven't had anything physical happen for a while, but I do once in a while get the shivers or feel cold for no reason. I think whatever is here is now satisfied just to watch me rather than mess with me."

Terri said she believes Shadow People are attracted to homes with conflict. "Domestic violence, alcohol, or drug abuse, or just a lot of arguing all the time," she said. "They get stronger when there are a lot of negative emotions present. They are psychic vampires. When you have one of these things attached to you, you frequently feel tired and depressed from them leeching your energy and emotions. These things are definitely not harmless. I wish I knew of some way to get rid of them."

The Stalking Hoard

The Shadow Man drifted from a corner of 13-year-old Jamie Shannon's room. She was in the twilight area of sleep, aware, but unable to move – and it was coming closer. "This seven-foot-tall Shadow in my room was dead set on keeping me in a sleep state," she said. "It was moving gradually toward my bed as I saw through my waking fight for consciousness."

The Shadow entity slid through her room, coming ever closer until he reached her bed and attacked her paralyzed form. "He shoved his arm into my throat," Shannon said. "My head filled with weird thoughts, I passed out, and woke up on the floor the next morning."

Shannon, now 26, has had many such experiences, as often as four to twelve times a week, over the past thirteen years. So she's observed repeated Shadow Person behavior. And it's not pretty. "Over the years I have noticed many things about them which I believe are starting to reveal itself as pack-hunting behavior," she said. "I have noticed that, number one, they are always in groups."

She's seen small Shadow People look into her room and feels those are scouts. "They peek in on you through windows, doorways, and never really come close enough to touch," she said. "Then they disappear or recede into the shadow of night cover."

These smaller Shadows are then followed by something larger, and more sinister. "The big one comes a while later," she said. "Between 2 and 5 a.m., though usually almost always at 3 a.m. sharp." The larger Shadows are the ones that freeze her to the bed. "This big one is the one with the disabling ability," she said. "The large ones I believed are the creatures used to disable prey for the pack. At first, I thought they potentially could have been the same group of Shadows, but there are literally thousands of them in any given city in the world and I am beginning to think that only [whose who are] especially 'aware' have the ability to see them, and in my case, open the minds of others to them."

They Are Demons

Something dark haunts a slow, quiet street in the small town of Folkston, Georgia. Most people don't realize this evil is in their midst, but gunsmith Eric London does. He's seen the creatures of this street, and he's felt their touch. "They are demons," Eric said. "They are demons who have not found a human host."

Eric has seen them out of the corner of his eye, Shadow People lurking in his home. "My former wife, a year before the divorce, was possessed by one of these," he said. "I was awakened by her jabbing me in the back while she was screaming at me, 'There is someone in the room.' I looked up and one of these solid black things was making its way quickly around the foot of our bed in the dim of the night."

As Eric jumped out of bed, he yelled for his wife to turn on the light. "I thought, at the time, it was a human breaking in. I was going for my handgun," Eric said. "She turns the light on by her bed, and has a real smart assed tone in her voice I had never heard before, 'whatcha doin'?'"

With the light on, the figure Eric and his wife had seen was gone. "I looked everywhere," he said. "I am really creeped out. She even says, 'He is not in there,' referring to a closet I was looking in."

Then Eric's life changed; the wife he knew no longer existed. Eric is convinced she was possessed by a demon that night. "We ended up divorced due to her buying an insurance policy, trying to kill me, telling me she never loved me, etc.," Eric said. "Do you think these Shadow People are harmless?"

Eric's ex-wife stopped communicating with him until she came to his house unannounced about a year later. "'They' entered unwelcome in to my home and told me she was coming back," Eric said, 'they' referring to his ex-wife and what Eric calls her demon. "When I said no, 'it' came part the way out of her face in a ghostlike manner. It made one hell of an ugly face and went back into her and she gathered up her purse and left."

"They" have not been back to Eric's house, but he has received a few telephone calls from his ex-wife and knows the demon is with her. "It still has her," he said. "I suffer grave guilt that I could not stop it. But I am told by many, I could not have anyway, but feelings are hard to deal with."

Even though his ex-wife is now gone from his life, he still sees these Shadow Demons. "I have seen them inside my home," he said, once while working at his computer. "I slowly moved my eyes to the side, and yes, it was a human-shaped solid black figure. It was totally startled to figure out I noticed. It faded away quickly."

But even more horrifying, he's *felt* the ones he hasn't seen. "I have actually been grabbed on three occasions so far, all within a month," Eric said. "I feel them move up from behind me, and on the first try I had one grab my bare calves." He felt icy fingers and a thumb grip each calf, spreading cold through his legs. "This angered me that they would rudely touch me," he said. "I told it to go away and it did." Other occurrences ended the same; Eric told the entity to leave, and it did.

He doesn't know why these entities have targeted him, but he knows how to make them leave. "Tell them to leave you alone," Eric said. "They are not aliens, not time travelers, not pleasant Disney characters. They are fucking demons."

CHAPTER 10

When Children See Shadows

Children often see things that aren't there, or at least, things we adults believe aren't there: an imaginary friend; a monster in the closet; a dark, human Shadow looming over their bed. Dr. Jackie Kibler, chair of the Department of Psychology, Sociology and Counseling at Northwest Missouri State University, said this is a phase called animistic thinking. "They give human-like qualities to inanimate objects. That's why shows like *Blue's Clues* appeal to them," she said. "This also allows them to create imaginary friends that they believe are real."

But do these misidentified, human-like figments of the imagination dredge terror from deep within children like it did to Danny? Darkness draped Danny's room as the 10-year-old fought to stay awake, the drone of his parents' television down the hall keeping sleep at bay. As he lay in bed, something – the feeling of safety – changed in his room. Danny was no longer alone. He lifted his head from the pillow and saw a human-shaped nightmare. "A tall Shadow bent over my top bunk bed as I squeezed my eyes shut and pretended to be asleep," Danny, now an adult, said. "But holy hell, it scared me half to death."

Children often see things adults don't; as parents rush into a room to see why their child cried out, they find nothing unusual. Medium Margie Kay, founder of the QUEST Investigation Group in Independence, Missouri, said this might be a result of societal conditioning. "Children just see the world as it is and have not yet been trained by society to see it differently," she said. "I think as people get older they just ignore the subtle part of their world, and also some people are admonished not to see these things because they must be evil, and so just delete it from their consciousness."

Psychic Shane Turnbeaugh agrees. "As a child I can remember hearing them laugh. It sounded much like a party going on in our kitchen. Except everyone in the house was sound asleep – besides me," Turnbeaugh said. "I can no longer hear the Shadow People and I assume that is just an ability I lost growing up."

Children, he said, are often very highly-tuned psychics: "Unfortunately, society teaches them to suppress most of it, so many people lose some or most of the abilities they are born with. Like any other human skill, I suppose you have to practice or you lose it."

Turnbeaugh remembers having the sense that the beings he was hearing and seeing then were merely "passing through" or "waiting" for something, but whatever these Shadow People were doing, most didn't seem to notice him. "Very seldom did any of them ever pay any attention to me," he said. "Though I can remember a few that would walk in front of my bedroom door and just watch me, as I watched back."

But many of these entities do interact with children. Brenda Marble, co-founder of Miller's Paranormal Research group, has witnessed this interaction firsthand. "Children will see ghosts up to a certain age," she said. Her four-year-old granddaughter once said she didn't want to go to grandma's house anymore because "there was a mean man there." Later, the girl accurately described the "mean man" – a biker who had just been buried in a cemetery adjacent to Marble's house.

Other paranormal investigators, and Darwin Linn, the owner of the haunted Axe Murder House in Villisca, Iowa, have witnessed children reacting to a presence invisible to adults in the room. During a paranormal investigation of the axe murder house, "a lady with a little girl came in and [the little girl] wanted to go in the other room," Darwin said. "It was dark there. Then this little boy did the same thing; he wanted to go in that room."

Darwin asked the psychic across the table from him why the children were doing this, "and she said [that children] are more open and they see kids in there and just want to play." Darwin looked into the room to see the children playing with someone – or some thing – he could not see.

A child's encounters with the paranormal could be psychological, or it could just be their age and an overactive imagination. It's common for young children to wake up screaming, terrified by something mom and dad can't see. Dr. April Haberyan, psychology professor at Northwest Missouri State University, said some of these events could be a psychological phenomenon called night terrors. "This typically [occurs] with children three to four," she said. "They're asleep, their eyes are open, they're screaming, but they don't remember anything. No detailed dream is recalled."

But, as the following encounters reveal, these children are often older than four, and they remember everything.

The Dark Man in My Room

When MaryAnn's son was four years old, he saw the Dark Man in his room. Because of a history of schizophrenia in MaryAnn's family, she was concerned for her son's mental health. That concern grew over the next five years as the dark, human-shaped Shadow increasingly brought terror into the boy's life.

"He always presented his encounters of this entity as something to fear," MaryAnn said. "I am a very rational person and I have little to no tolerance for the inane fears of people who seem to be 'taken in' by the paranormal."

MaryAnn tried to convince her son that the Shadow Man lurking in his room could be rationalized away, but he continued to see it. "He is almost 12 years old now, yet recalls the encounters as though they happened yesterday," MaryAnn said. "He is as adamant that these were real encounters as he was years ago when he was trying to convince me they were happening. I was sure then that he believed his experiences to be real. Now I am left to consider whether they actually were real."

My Son's Shadows

Julie's military family moved often, as military families are prone to do. But when she was about seven years old, they settled into a house that would haunt her for years. "I experienced Shadow People as a child," she said. "I would see, night after night, people [of] all shapes and sizes walking down our hallway."

But these weren't people, she said – they were Shadows. "I remember looking for the source day after day to try and explain what I was seeing." But she never found one.

Julie would also hear music the rest of her family could not, and she played with people they could not see. "My mother tells me I had a whole town of 'imaginary' friends," she said. "Those I only remember slightly and only names."

As an adult, Julie stands helpless as Shadow People visit her son. "He sees people walking down the hall, and he wants his door shut," she said. "I believe him because of what I saw – it was the same." Julie experienced dark figures walking up stairs and standing in her hallway.

Julie's son – now with his mother in a new house – is terrified. "He hasn't been afraid of anything before," she said. "But he is here. Now he's afraid of the dark."

Dad Saw the Shadow

In 1989, a tall, black Shadow woke eight-year-old John of Wisconsin, to a night of terror. "I was sleeping in my room and I could feel something pushing the bed in my sleep," John said. He awoke and noticed that a dark figure was standing at the end of the bed. "It was dark in my room, but this figure was so dark it just stood out. This thing was the darkest shade of black I have ever seen; so much that in a pitch black room it still stands out because it is so black. It was a perfect shape of a man." John finished sleeping the night with his parents.

But that wasn't the end of the Shadow Man in John's life. A few weeks after his encounter, his parents had an argument, so John's father slept in his room and John slept on the couch. "Everyone was sleeping when I awoke to a scream," he said. "A few minutes later I heard my mom and dad talking at the kitchen table. [When] my dad was sleeping [he had] felt someone pushing at the end of the bed. He woke up and saw a man."

John has never discovered who this Shadow Man was, but he had an idea what it was. "I don't know if it's evil or just mischievous," he said, "but I don't think it's a friendly spirit."

The Shadow Under the Bed

Something pulled nine-year-old Keri from sleep one night in late 1988 – something that shouldn't have been in her room. "I woke up in the middle of the night out of nowhere and looked at the foot of my bed to see a smoky, dark 'thing' slowly moving across from my right to left," Kerri said. "It was about four and a half to five feet tall with noticeable vapors trailing off its body."

Curious, Keri watched the black thing that was "much darker" than the darkness of her room. "As it got to the left corner of my bed, it stopped moving and turned its 'head' to look at me," she said. "It just stood there for a moment, and I could actually see it move its head closer, as if it were trying to see whether or not I was looking at it."

Through the darkness, the Shadow saw what it suspected – that Keri was aware of it. "Once it saw I was looking at it, it quickly dove down under my bed in a blink of an eye," she said. "I hurried up and looked under my bed to see if I could see it, but all I saw was darkness."

Keri then stood and felt for the light switch. Seconds later, light filled the room and Keri again looked under the bed. "I saw nothing," she said. "The feeling I had was as if I had surprised it just as much as it surprised me."

My Sister Saw It, Too

The Farris family moved into their first home in Kansas City, Missouri, in the early 1970s. Through stacks of boxes and the slow process of unpacking, five-year-old Danny found his way to the basement and discovered someone there with him. "When I went down there, I saw a Shadowy silhouette of a man walk along the wall opposite of the windows," said Danny, who watched the figure slide through the room with its back against the wall.

"He acted as if he was afraid of me," Danny said. "At the time I was not afraid, but bewildered. I told my mother of this, and it was dismissed as a child's imagination."

But Danny knew otherwise, especially after he saw the Shadow Man for the second time. "I was awakened that night by a loud crash seemingly coming from our kitchen," Danny said. "As I laid there in the middle of the night, I saw the silhouette of a man walk down the hallway passing my open door going towards my infant sister's room."

His sister would eventually confirm for him the reality of the Shadow Man. "It would be easy to dismiss these events as the overactive imagination of a child, but as my sightings diminished my sister began to tell my mother of the same types of sightings," Danny said. "I remember her asking my Mom if she could have a Halloween costume like the dress with lights that the lady who comes into her room at night wears."

Danny had seen this Shadow Woman himself; it was one of his last encounters before the entities left him. "Maybe children have the ability to see things adults can't," he said. "I lost the ability to see them while my little sister continued to see them for a few more years. Who knows, maybe you could have these things in your house right now."

The Hand Under the Bed

There was something wrong with Stephanie Wentz's grandmother's house. "There was something about her house that always didn't seem right in the back of my head," she said. Wentz, now 16, was six and on a sleepover when she discovered why.

Wentz slept on a twin-sized bed with her grandmother because she didn't like sleeping alone in that house. "[My grandmother] got up in the middle of the night and went to use the bathroom," she said. "I woke up when she got up and was very alert. I rolled over and let my arm hang over the bed as she went to the bathroom."

Light from a cracked-open bathroom door cut through the space between her grandmother and grandfather's twin beds. Wentz lay there, staring lazily at her arm when something grabbed her wrist. "In the light I could clearly see a hand blacker than the darkest night grabbing my arm and attempting to pull me down onto the floor," she said. "The whole time it touched my arm I didn't feel skin on me. I felt fear and dread coming from the hand."

Wentz tried to scream, but no noise came from her throat. "I only stared at the hand trying to pull me," she said. "Somehow, a basic instinct I guess, I pulled my arm away and it let go. I scooted back and pushed my back to the wall because the bed was up against a wall. When my grandma returned I held her tightly and began to cry."

Her grandmother asked why she was crying, but she wouldn't answer. As sleep tugged at Wentz, she drifted off in terror. "The most frightening thing about this whole experience is [when] I had begun going back to sleep, I sensed something in the corner of the ceiling right above my head," she said. "I suddenly began fearing the night-time."

Wentz began seeing Shadow People standing by the closet or looming over the bed watching her. "A dense, almost paralyzing pressure would close in on me and the sense of dread washed over me every time the lights went out," she said. "That happened every night, but slowly I began to live with the fear."

Morphing Shadows

As a huddle of boys rustled in the yard across from a retirement home, one of them saw balls of light dancing in a tree. "I started seeing things when I was younger and they scared the hell out of me," Patrick said. "I know [the balls of light] were real. My friends...all saw it, too."

But the dancing orbs of light weren't Patrick's last encounter with the paranormal. "Later on, this lady would visit my room every night in my closet and stare," he said. "She had no eyes, just black sockets, always floating around a foot off the ground. Very menacing to a twelve year old."

The eyeless woman was only the first of many visitors in his room – and not the worst. "In the same house I saw Shadow Figures in the mirror next to my bed," he said. "They actually shook my bed one night. I saw them in the mirror peeking under my covers."

For years, Patrick tried to explain away these terrifying encounters, but they chased him into adulthood.

"As an adult, they actually come to me and present themselves," he said. "But they change their shape and expressions so fast it's hard to tell what's what."

A study of children newborn to 11 years old, completed September 19, 2006, by Nicole Leader for Ghoststudy.com, found children, more than adults, are likely to see ghosts. They seem to lose that ability after years of adult discouragement. So don't discount children's ghost stories as the product of their imagination. They see more than we know.

CHAPTER 11

Cats and other Shadow Animals

Small things move in sixteen-year-old Stephanie Wentz's house. Small, quick, black things. "When I'm laying on my bed reading or watching television, I notice a small flash of black in the corner of my eyes, like something is running past my bed," she said. "At first I think it's my black cat, but when I see him, he's in a completely different area in the room." Although the moving Shadows are not her cat, she's certain the quick, black figure is a cat. "In the corner of my eye, I always see a slinky little tail or a little black body running behind my chair or the front of my bed," she said.

Cats and the paranormal have been intertwined for centuries. During the Middle Ages, cats were thought to be spirit familiars that served and guarded witches, and cats were often burned alive with their masters who were deemed to be practicing the dark art of witchcraft. Witches, it was thought, could also assume the shape of cats and would sneak into to the room of a sleeping infant to rob them of their life. Many witches confessed to this during the witch trials, although most did not confess without torture.

Satan is also thought to take the earthly form of a black cat. Paranormal investigator and author Alexandra Gargiulo said that although Shadows do take the form of animals, they are probably animal spirits and are not as devilish as they sound. "Animals are also part of apparitions and will never cause any harm," she said. "They're doing what they would have done in life to their previous owners or whereabouts."

These Shadow Cats have been seen in many cultures, but why cats? Why not dogs, monkeys, or cows? Wahde, a Cherokee, said medicine people who have turned evil (referred to as sgili, or witches) will use the shape of a dark animal to attack others. "Some of the medicine people who we consider shape shifters can take that form," he said. "Owls, foxes, ravens, wolves. And they can look like other things, like Shadow People."

Bishop James Long, pastor of St. Christopher Old Catholic Church in Louisville, Kentucky, said there are all sorts of Shadow animals, but the cat means something specific – and ominous. "Quite often, you will see animals of all types that are described as a black Shadow," he said. "The cat tends to be the result of dark witchcraft. Dark or black witchcraft is most certainly real, and I have witnessed several animal shapes that evil entities will try to imitate."

The Demon Cat of the Capitol Building in Washington, D.C., might fit Bishop Long's description. People have reported seeing this cat in the basement crypt near the raised platform where a dead president's casket rests. The cat usually appears before a change in office or a president's death. This small black cat with glowing yellow eyes seems to grow before attacking its startled victim.

The Lion of Darkness

Lindsie Harlan of Austin, Texas, woke in the early morning hours to find a visitor in her room, a swirling, smoky cloud that slowly coalesced into the head of a lion. "I woke up and I looked toward my door," she said. "I didn't even realize I was looking at anything until I saw these huge eyes staring at me. It was this swirling vortex of a cloud with two huge eyes. It had a mouth – and it was open. It looked more like a human mouth on a lion head with huge eyes. I was afraid, terrified."

Lindsie muttered, "Oh, my God, go away, go away, go away, go away, please go away," and the apparition slowly disappeared, leaving her in the cold, dark room. "I turned on my lamp and could actually see my chest move from my heart pounding," she said. "It was beating fast for maybe 30 minutes. I couldn't calm down. I panicked. I felt nothing but evil coming off of that thing."

Attacked by a Shadow Cat

Max and his cousin sat in the darkness on the back steps of the house. The sounds of laughter poured from inside the house, a party for Max's uncle nearing full crescendo. As they sat in the tungsten glow from windows that bathed the yard in a dissipating yellow, they could make out the fence that lined the property.

But Max and his cousin wished they hadn't. "We noticed a Shadow creeping along the fence," Max said. "I guess it noticed it was being watched and stopped. It was hunched over like it was trying to be covert."

The boys stared at a black, cat-shaped Shadow in curiosity, but the curiosity quickly faded into terror. "It turned its head to look at us," Max said. "It had bright yellow eyes. As soon as it looked at us, it turned and ran into the shadows." They ran inside.

What was the creeping Shadow in the back yard? Max didn't know, but it wasn't his last encounter with a Shadow Cat. "A Shadow Cat used to live with me in my apartment," he said. "It was very mean when I moved in." Walking through his apartment, Max would often feel the thing pouncing on him. "It would be on my back, scratching me," he said.

But after a while, the attacks slowly stopped. "It grew on me, and I liked having it around," Max said. "I guess it was mad that I moved in."

The Shadow Menagerie

Shadows walk. Whether on the street or in her home, Janice Tremeear knows the Shadows are there – she sees them. "Since childhood, I've seen Shadow People and other things: faces, figures, heard voices, felt unseen presences, etc.," Janice, of Springfield, Missouri, said. Now, as an adult, she sees the dead standing by their loved ones. She can describe their appearance and clothing and family members confirm her descriptions. "These were people I did not know," she said.

But since she was a child, the most prevalent entity in her life has been the Shadow Person. "It's something I've accepted and lived with all my life," she said. "I've seen the adult human sized, smaller human shapes, rat and cat sizes/shapes and a few shapes that stay along the top of the wall near the ceiling, almost like crows."

In December 2006, Janice's boyfriend visited her home near Kansas City, Missouri, when he saw the Shadows, too. "He was startled to see a dark cat shape run across my kitchen," she said. "I did not have any pets, as he well knew. It was simply one of the Shadow animals that always seem to be around me."

Janice never felt threatened by these Shadows until her daughter brought one home. "A few years ago, one of my daughters and a school buddy of hers went to the Devil's Tunnel near Warrenton, Missouri, where we lived at that time," she said.

Devil's Tunnel, also called Satan's Tunnel, is part of an abandoned railway line supposedly haunted by the ghost of a drifter killed by a train. "They both experienced something that terrified them and came home very frightened."

On this warm summer night, Janice had left the front door open and when the girls explained their encounter, Janice saw something through that door – something bad. "I saw a man-sized black shape lurking about just beyond my driveway," she said. "I had the feeling the girls had been followed home, but the Shadow did not or could not come any closer to the house."

Janice, her daughter, and her friend watched the Shadow Being stand at the end of the drive – it was staring at them. "Both girls were very frightened by the thing," she said. "It hung around outside for awhile. There was a streetlight nearby, so it was easy to see."

Janice told it to go away, that it wasn't allowed on her property. Later, the Shadow walked off. "So far the only threatening Shadow I've encountered was the one who appeared to have followed my daughter and her friend home from Devil's Tunnel," Janice said. "It's hard to say why that figure seemed a threat, just a feeling or the posture of the thing. It did seem to be staring in at us and aware we were there in the house."

Most of the Shadows, Janice said, feel like old friends or curious passersby, and there are some comforting paranormal figures in Janice's home – the Shadow Cats. "It does appear that a few of the cat shapes behave like a pet," she said. "And they too are aware of me and like being around me."

The Transforming Shadow

The Shadow Man follows Dee Jay Schmidt's 10-year-old son Dan everywhere: to school, a friend's house, and around his own home. Dee Jay sees it, too, but for her it's different. "I've seen these things forever, even felt a couple," she said. "I'm use to them, but my son has one that follows him and scares him to death."

At first, the Shadow Man would jump out from behind things like it was playing with Dan. But the boy didn't think it was a game when the entity visited him every week and, more frighteningly, every day. "My son asks it to go away every time it shows up," she said.

The Shadow is not always a man. Sometimes it appears as something more friendly. "My son is obsessed with cats, and this figure will occasionally transform into a Shadow Cat rather than a Shadow Person," she said. "Last week, my son said it made a hissing sound as it tried to say something. He said it sounded part snake and was trying to say 'Hey.'"

The boy closed his eyes and told it to go away. "Then the toy he had in his hand jumped out and hit him in his chest," she said – and the creature was gone. "I'm use to them and they don't bother me anymore. But my son is terrified."

Grandma's Cat

Darren was spending a few days with his grandmother in 1989, when one night something jumped on his bed. "I was sleeping in my [deceased] grandfather's bed," he said. "I was just getting ready to fall asleep when the cat jumped onto the foot of my bed, quite lightly."

Darren then remembered that dogs had killed his grandmother's cat a few months before his visit. "With that realization, I immediately sat up and saw the form of my grandfather standing at the foot of the bed," he said. The form stood, details clouded in darkness, but Darren was certain he was seeing his dead grandfather. "I told my grandmother in the morning, and her eyes opened up real wide and in her High German accent she screamed, 'Aaaaaaa.'"

Later, she told Darren she thought she was going crazy, because she had seen the Shadow of her dead husband, too.

The Shadow Cat had Blazing Red Eyes

The old brownstone apartment in downtown Chicago had been recently remodeled. In 2002, Dan Bryce lived on the second floor. He shared it with his cat – and something dark. "Around this time, I began to catch fleeting glimpses of a small black cat," he said. "The cat was only visible in my peripheral vision, and if I tried to look at it directly it would disappear."

Dan brushed off these sightings of the tiny Shadow Cat as his mind playing tricks. Besides, he had a mostly black male cat in his apartment, so he was used to seeing something small and dark slink around.

Then one night he realized that this Shadow Cat wasn't his imagination. "One evening I had a strange encounter with this Shadow Cat that led me to realize that this is some sort of entity," he said. "It was late in the evening and I went into my bedroom to get ready for bed. As I bent over to unlace my boots, I noticed the small dark cat had walked up and stopped at the base of the dresser, just inches away from my feet."

Dan could only see the Shadow Cat from the corner of his eye, but this startled him because the creature had never ventured so close to him. "I had never previously acknowledged the Shadow Cat's presence, but since it was so close, I said, 'Oh, hello,'" he said. He snapping his head toward the Shadow Cat to catch it in his full vision, but suddenly, the Shadow Cat was gone.

"It was almost like the motion blur of a camera," he said. "At first I looked around thinking maybe there is a stray cat that snuck into the apartment." Dan quickly dismissed that thought; there was no way for a stray cat to get in.

But the fleeting glimpse of the Shadow Cat by his dresser did answer one question – it was not his cat. "It was definitely not my cat," he said. "This cat was tiny, almost kitten-sized, while my cat weighed nearly 16 pounds."

Dismissing this intruder cat, Dan changed into nightclothes, grabbed a book and settled into bed. "I figured, okay, I'm just over-tired," he said. Then he noticed his cat slink through the crack in his partially opened door – and it was stalking something Dan couldn't see.

"He often slept on my bed, especially during the colder months," Dan said. "The bedroom was tiny so I thought this would be a good opportunity to see if my cat could detect anything unusual in the room. At this point, I was very calm and relaxed. After all, I considered the Shadow Cat to be nothing more than a figment of my imagination."

Dan's cat slowly approached the bed then froze. "He turned and looked back at the dresser where the Shadow Cat had stood."

Dan watched in fascination as his cat assumed a stalking position and approached the dresser. "He slowly circled the dresser and climbed underneath," Dan said. "I had never before seen my cat go under the dresser as it is very low to the floor, and he literally had to crawl and remain on his belly while under there."

Dan almost expected to hear a catfight, but a few minutes later, his cat crawled from beneath the dresser. "Again, he circled back and forth in front of the dresser and laid down on the floor placing himself between me and the dresser. He continued to watch that spot as I turned off the lights and went to sleep," Dan said. "I was very impressed with my cat, and felt sure he was protecting me, even though I felt no malice from the [Shadow] creature."

That was the last time Dan saw the Shadow Cat in Chicago, but the Shadow Cat wasn't finished with him. A few months later, Dan moved out of Chicago and into an old building in rural southeastern Wisconsin. His cat made the move with him, but so had the Shadow Cat. "I was surprised to find that the Shadow Cat had followed us," he said. "Though not as frequent, I could still catch glances of him creeping about."

Then, one night, Dan's Shadow Cat turned sinister. "As I slept, I awoke suddenly to find this cat on my bed staring at me," he said. "This time I could see him perfectly, sitting right in front of me – a small black cat, but his eyes blazed red. Although I could still feel no malice coming from the creature, I was frightened by his demonic appearance."

Terrified, Dan's hands shot to the creature's throat, but something was wrong. "I noticed that my arms were translucent and glowed a pale blue," he said. "I began to tighten my grip around the creature's throat. I did not know what this thing was, but I did not want it around any longer. I would kill it if I could."

Then, Dan realized he might still be sleeping, and he might be hurting his own cat. "I released my grip on the Shadow Cat and immediately woke up," he said. "I sat up in the dark; no Shadow Cats, and my cat was not even in the room."

Was Dan's experience a dream, or more than a dream? "If it was a dream, the Shadow Cat certainly got the message," he said. "That was over two years ago, and even though I still catch a glimpse of this cat once in awhile, it now keeps a safe distance from me."

Dan's cat died at the age of 16. "He was a true friend," Dan said. "I have since taken in a female stray. Now if I can only teach her to guard against the Shadows."

My Cat Came Back

For the six years James' cat lived in his family's home, it slept on the foot of his bed. "It was my best friend," James said. "It was a loyal pet that I'm not afraid to say that I cared a great deal for."

After a long illness, James' family put the cat down in 1991. "He had a condition that just wasn't going to get any better," James said. "But it didn't feel as if his presence left after his passing." Something was sleeping on his bed.

"There was one night after he was gone that I awoke to feel him sleeping at the foot of my bed," he said. "I didn't move. I didn't look. I just felt the comfort of having my old friend around again, if only for one night. He never did this again."

But some entity remained in the home. "My family would always get little indications that this cat wasn't necessarily gone," he said. "We'd be sitting, watching TV, and would see a Shadow Cat run by in the corner of one's eye. It was just as a cat, my cat, used to do."

The family took these signs as comfort that their cat wasn't really gone, but when they brought home another cat in early 1992, they found the Shadow Cat didn't want it there. "This cat spent the first night with us sleeping at the foot of my bed, just as our other cat used to do," James said. "[But] he only did this one night – never again."

The Shadow Cat may have chased its successor throughout the house. "This newer cat would constantly run past us in the same general direction that the phantom cat would run," James said. "It always appeared to be getting chased or bothered by something that wasn't there. It took some time, but eventually these phantom occasions disappeared altogether."

Other Shadow Animals

Melissa Styles has always been sensitive to the unseen world around her. "I'm very sensitive to feelings," she said. "Certain houses make me uncomfortable to be in."

One such house was the one in New Jersey where she grew up. "My grandfather bought it and the previous owner had fallen down the steps and broken her neck," she said. The family dog wouldn't go upstairs or into any of the back rooms, the thermostat would change the setting by itself, and Styles never felt alone in the apartment upstairs.

"You would be sitting in the living room, and there was a loft above me, and I'd sit there and would just know something was standing up at the top of that loft looking at me," she said. "I'd never look. That particular house just had a lot of stuff going on." Like the Shadow Animals.

"This all happened when I was about four," she said. "This, to me, completely happened." While four-year-old Styles was in bed, a procession of Shadows shaped like animals filed through her room. "I saw it every single night for a long time," she said. "I would see these Shadows, these shapes, of animals. I remember a gorilla – a line of them."

These Shadow animals, one of which was a giraffe three or four feet high, walked past her bed and always went into the bathroom. "I remember the gorilla walking on his knuckles, a knuckle swing. It was a constant line. Laying there watching this I thought this was crazy," she said. "I'd see it. I'd pee the bed. And I'd have to explain it to my mom. I never went into the bathroom."

Although she hasn't seen these Shadow Animals for decades, the thought of them still gives her chills. "It was scary," she said. "It wasn't a 'you're scared for your life' scary. It wasn't horror. But anything you can't explain is scary."

The Hairball, the Spider, and the Demons

Stephan Jansen of London is no stranger to the paranormal. His great grandfather on his father's side was an African witchdoctor, and his grandmother on his mother's side could foresee the death of family members weeks before it happened.

So, when Jansen lived in South Africa, he wasn't at all afraid when he saw animal-shaped Shadow creatures – including a featureless "hairball" – skitter about the room. "At the time, magic and curses were thrown from one family member to the other, and my life was a mess," he said. "The hairball always kept to the corners of the room when someone was [there]. He was there before the house became a hotbed of curses, and it was only after the curses started that he tore the carpet up under my bed. Maybe the spiritual energy hurt or frustrated him."

But, nothing touched him physically until he encountered the spider. "Out of all the shapes of Shadows that I have seen, only one has had the guts to attack so far," he said. "It was in the shape of a spider, and crawled up the wall at breakneck speed, to above my bed, and then dropped straight on top of me. I jumped from the fright, as I did not expect it, but escaped fairly unharmed from it."

One Shadow shaped like a cat would toy with Jansen. "It would wait for me to come through the front door, and make sure that I saw it," he said. "As no pets were allowed in my parents' house, I would chase it all the way into my parents bedroom, where it would just disappear. This happened several times until proper demons moved in."

That's when the atmosphere in the Jansen house became "heavy, as if the air is very humid and you struggle to breathe," and dark, "as if there was no sunshine coming in, even though all the windows were open." Pets – real, not Shadows – would mysteriously die in the night. Jansen's family finally called for help, and the demonic activity – including the mystery Shadow animals – disappeared. "The house had to be cleansed by a witchdoctor in the end."

CHAPTER 12

The Hat Man

The bride and groom awoke with a start. They were honeymooning in St. Louis at the Lemp Mansion Bed and Breakfast, a stately white, three-story, 33-room home near the Anheuser-Busch Brewing Company. The mansion was built by beer baron William J. Lemp in the 1860s. Over the decades, the mansion absorbed the misery of a once great family devastated by Prohibition and was home to multiple mysterious deaths and suicides – including, Frederick Lemp, William J. Lemp, William J. Lemp, Jr., William Lemp III, Charles Lemp, and Charles' beloved Doberman pinscher. Now the mansion houses a restaurant, bed and breakfast, and permanent guests – guests that wander the mansion silently in the night.

"The bride and groom said they had an uneasy feeling and awoke and saw an outline of a person at the end of their bed with a top hat on," Mary Wolff, director of operations at the Lemp Mansion said. "As quickly as they could focus, there was no one in the room."

This dark, top hat wearing Shadow has been seen before. "In 1975, when my father purchased this building, we got a letter from someone in Arkansas says he saw a ghost here in the mid-60s," Wolff said. "He said he was going down the hallway late at night and saw a top-hatted figure with a cape on the stairs. He noted he had really shiny shoes."

Wolff believes the Lemp Mansion's Shadowy Hat Man is probably the ghost of Charles Lemp: "[He was] very dapper and very fastidious." But there are reports of this type of Shadow Entity from across the world wearing everything from a top hat to a derby to – what seems to be the most common – a fedora. What, then, are these hat-wearing Shadow People?

The Hat Man's behavior mirrors that of most Shadow People reports – a black, two-dimensional Shadow of a slightly out-of-proportion man walking with some purpose – but why the hat? Paranormal investigator Alexandra Gargiulo, like Wolff, is convinced these hat-wearing Shadow People are the souls of the not-to-dearly departed. "These are ghosts who were not good in their earthly lives and passed horribly," she said. "They were soulless and in the stuck realm of the living, they continue to haunt areas, places, and people continuing their bad ways. Many souls that have passed are stuck. Ghosts can show themselves anyway they see fit including wearing a signature hat or garment."

But the Hat Man may be a cultural manifestation – people are seeing what the literature of the time is telling them to see. Dr. Bryn H. Gribben, a professor of 19th century British literature at Northwest Missouri State University, said ghostly Shadows often serve as a literary tool that reflect the fears of the time: "Usually authors are depicting ghosts as a symbol. In *The Shadow in the Corner* by Mary Elizabeth Braddon, it's just this weeping figure that just hangs around until the ethically right thing is done." Most of Braddon's Shadows are female, because female apparitions were more frightening to the male-dominated culture of the Victorian era.

But these Shadow figures in literature come and go as cultural problems change. "The 18th century is the Age of Reason so you don't see ghosts in literature," Gribben said. "The supernatural reappeared in the Romantic Period. In 20th century England, they have an absence in ghosts because they had so many things to worry about: World War I, World War II, the end of the Empire. There's too much anxiety to deal with. It's almost like ghosts are for leisure time."

The Hat Man, Gribben said, may relate to business-men. In a world ruled by corporations, this may not be far off. Dr. Karla Edwards, psychology professor at Northwest Missouri State University, agrees that this creeping black, hat-wearing figure we see in our periphery accompanied by feelings of impending doom probably reflects society's fears. "Culturally, it's so common I'm not surprised [the Hat Man] shows up," she said. "But, you know, I would have thought horns would be more common."

However, those who see the hat-wearing Shadow Man don't consider its cultural implications, they're just afraid of the black thing lurking in their house.

Stalked by Shadows

Although Sarah Kelly has never seen the Hat Man, her mother and grandmother weren't so lucky. "My mom and my grandma have always told me about this spirit that was following them wherever they moved," she said. "In the beginning, they would both hear heavy breathing beneath my mom's bed when she was little." Then, one night the monster came out from under the bed. "A tall man in a long coat with no face and black holes for eyes wearing some sort of hat. Luckily I've never experienced that but it still gives me chills."

The Dark Man on the Stairs

There was something on Angie's stairs. Nights when her children stayed with their father, or were asleep in their rooms and Angie was downstairs alone – always alone – the Dark Man would come. "I always called him the Dark Man on the Stairs," Angie said. "That's where I saw him, coming down the stairs."

The first night of what became an 18-month ritual at first caught Angie off guard. "I'm an adult," she said. "I thought, 'did I just see that?' The first time it kind of

141

creeped me out, but it didn't scare me."

She never saw the Shadow Man anywhere but on the stairs, and his routine never varied. "I would catch him from the landing down the last couple of stairs, then to the left toward the kitchen," she said. "And it was distinctly a man. It was a man in a suit with a hat."

The Shadow Man looked like someone from the 1930s who was dressed for church, but Angie got that impression from his black outline, as she could make out no features. "But it was very distinctly a man," she said.

As the Dark Man turned to walk into the kitchen, he would vanish. "It would just kind of disappear," she said. "I never actually saw him entering the kitchen. I saw him, for lack of a better word, vaporize. I never saw him get past the dining room but definitely he was going somewhere."

As Angie grew used to the Dark Man, something happened that eventually drove her to move her family from the house – her five-year-old son woke up screaming. "He saw a group of people in his room," Angie said. "I didn't see them. All I know is he woke up screaming and I heard him screaming really hysterical. He was sitting up in his bed and the look on his face frightened me to no end. I asked what was wrong and he said, 'get rid of them – all these people.' That did scare me."

Her son, now a high school student, vaguely remembers the incident, but can't remember who the people were or what they looked like. "I remember saying 'what people?' And he said, 'make them go away,'" Angie said. "I firmly believed he saw people in his room."

Just as she's sure she saw the Dark Man. "Some people dismiss them as electrical impulses in your brain," Angie said. "Then why have I not had these electrical impulses everywhere I've lived? Why just in this house? I'm not crazy. I saw him. I would swear on a stack of Bibles. I'm an intelligent woman. I know what I saw."

I'm Not Crazy

Shadows lurked in the corners of Jenni Lee's home and her mind as she battled depression. "I was in a seriously depressed state," she said. "I started seeing Shadows out of the corner of my eyes. I really thought it had something to do with the emotional state I was in [and that they were] hallucinations." Until one night when she was up late, around 11 p.m., talking with a friend over the internet when she noticed a large, black Shadow moving out of the corner of her right eye. "I was about to mention it to the friend I was talking to, but as soon as I turned back around from looking to my right, there it was, two feet in front of me on a wall behind the computer monitor," she said.

A Shadow Man stood out from the wall directly in front of her. "No longer was it an illusion from the corner of my eye," she said. "It was only a matter of seconds and it had whisked away across the wall while fading."

There was nothing human about its movement; in the time it took her to blink, it shot across the wall and disappeared. "It was a Shadow figure of a larger man with a dated fedora hat and what appeared to be a cloak," she said. "I froze. Not able to look behind me, I made a mad dash straight towards the bedroom."

Shaking and scared, she woke her boyfriend Josh and explained what she saw. "He's a deep sleeper and fell right back to sleep leaving me with nothing but my thoughts," she said. "Was I crazy?"

The next day, Jenni Lee began an internet search for her fedora-wearing Shadow Man, and she discovered she was not alone – many people have seen this entity. "I typed in 'Shadow Men' in a...search engine, and the first picture I saw was an almost exact depiction of the Shadow Man I saw," she said. "They called him 'Hat Man.' Then I started thinking I wasn't so crazy. After talking to several people about this experience, I found that many people I know have had a very similar experience."

Followed by Shadows

The paranormal seems to follow certain people and Mary Vincent of Kingston, Ontario, is one of them. At the age of 17, Mary was staying with her brother when she realized something in his house wasn't right. "I was sleeping in a loft-type bedroom," she said. "I woke suddenly one night with the immediate knowledge I wasn't alone."

Sitting at the side of her bed, staring at her, was a man. "He just sat very still and the darkness of the room wouldn't allow me to see his face," she said. "It seemed as if he had a hat on. I was totally terrified. I tried to move but found I couldn't. I couldn't even turn my head away."

From her bed, she tried to scream for help, but could only manage a whisper. Then, as quickly as she'd noticed the Shadow Man, he was gone. "I lay there scared and shaken," she said.

The next morning, she didn't talk about her encounter, nor the next day, nor the next. "I did not tell anybody about this for years," she said. "I didn't want to hear 'you were dreaming' when I knew I wasn't."

The Broken Window

The tumor was large, about the size of a chicken egg. In the spring of 1971, a surgeon removed the cancerous mass from 11-year-old Rob Langevoort's brain and Rob spent months undergoing radiation therapy. So, when Rob started seeing things that didn't belong in his home, he didn't know if they were real or imaginary.

His first encounter took place on a summer Saturday in 1971. With his mom out shopping, and his dad repairing rental property, Rob had their home in Niskayuna, N.Y., to himself. "I proceeded down the hall to the kitchen to make myself something to eat for breakfast [and]

I fell flat on my face," Rob said. "It felt as though I was pushed."

Rob tried to push himself up but couldn't move – he felt someone standing on his back. "All of a sudden things gave way and my arms had straightened out and I was staring down the hall to the living room just in time to witness what appeared to be a silhouette of a man in a trench coat wearing a fedora move from the living room to the dining room," he said. Rob would later call this entity the Hat Man.

Despite the attack, Rob followed it. "What I did next I find hard to believe," he said. "I ran into the adjoining kitchen, grabbed the biggest knife I could find, and ran into the dining room."

The Hat Man wasn't there. The sliding glass door that led from the dining room to the back porch was still closed, the drapes covering it hung still. He ran through the house and found himself alone, clenching a knife. All the doors and windows were locked.

"I searched that house good," he said. "Nothing. I went back to the dining room and checked the sliding glass door again. It was locked." Since he hadn't heard the front door open, the back porch was the only way out. He unlocked the sliding glass door and stepped onto the porch, thinking the Hat Man had somehow locked the sliding door behind him and leapt off the porch. But 10 feet below the porch railing was rock – and that was the only way down. "My father had the builders purposely not install a stairway up to the porch to prevent any intrusions," Rob said. The Hat Man was gone, and he didn't jump off the porch.

Was the Hat Man real, or just a side effect of the brain tumor? Rob wondered. "What exactly did I see, or did I see it?" he asked. "And how am I gonna tell Mom?"

Rob's mother listened to his story and filed it away as a product of radiation or an overactive 11-year-old mind – until she saw the handiwork of the Hat Man herself.

Seven days later, "my mother prepared breakfast in the dining room, opened the drapes, and got the shock of her life," Rob said. "The sliding glass door was shattered." The entire six-foot glass door had been broken into small pieces. Not by a projectile from outside the house, but from something inside. Only the interior of the double-pane glass was shattered. Rob was sure the Hat Man had been hiding inside the door.

Although Rob hasn't seen the Hat Man since he was 11, he's seen similar Shadow Beings all his life, although nothing has pushed him or broken glass in decades. Now an internet programmer with two children, Shadow People remain a part of his life. "I still see them after 30-plus years and more often now since I have moved in with my elderly father," Rob said. "It's not disturbing to me other than they won't stay still long enough for me to take a good look at them. They appear as semi-transparent charcoal gray foggy silhouettes that I catch in the corner of my eye."

When Rob tries to look at them straight on, they zip away. "I see them mostly in doorways and hallways," Rob said. "I saw one once dash around a sofa. This tells me they can see objects – probably including me. I don't get excited, [they're] pretty commonplace with me after all these years. How often do I see these Shadow People? All the time."

I Know They're Evil

Murphy was eight years old when the Shadow Man brought terror into his home. "When I began to have encounters, I first felt scared for no reason; then out of nowhere the Shadow image appeared," he said. "It resembled a Batman cartoon character, only it was wearing a dress hat." The creature appeared to being wearing a suit, and it had sharp white eyes.

For Murphy, now in his mid-20s, the encounters

have continued. "There are three types that I have seen," he said. "The [Hat Man], the second Shadow entity has a round head, is thinner, and has glowing red eyes that looked like glowing red lights. The others had no legs and seemed to fly around in the air."

The worst encounters have occurred while he's in bed. "My bedroom is pitch black, but I can still see that black Shadow Figure because it is darker than the pitch-black bedroom," he said. "When they appear in my bedroom, it is almost as if I am paralyzed. I know these beings are evil because before they appear, I feel scared for no reason."

Murphy has found the only way to rid his night of Shadows is to turn on his bedroom light, but he just wants to know what these Shadows want. "These beings always come out at night between the hours of midnight and 5 a.m.," Murphy said. "But I don't know what these beings are, or why they are following me."

The Derby

Corky Simpson, a writer with the *Tucson Citizen*, and his wife were staying in the Louisa May Alcott Room of the Grand Avenue Bed and Breakfast in Carthage, Missouri, when they were visited in the night. "I woke up one night, and I'm not pulling your leg," Corky said. "I thought, geez, I'm looking at a streetlight, but I don't remember there being a streetlight out there. I went to go back to sleep and the light didn't go away."

That's because there is no streetlight outside the windows of that room. But Corky saw something more than a light. "I saw the outline of this guy who had a cigar," he said. "It wasn't a frightening thing at all. It was like a person with backlighting. He seemed to be an older fella and he was smoking a cigar. It seemed to me like he had a derby or something, but I couldn't tell. It had the vague outline of a very high collar – something that would have been worn at the turn of the century. The most amazing part to me is that this wasn't something that frightened you. It was just there. You had a sense of serenity. It was like meeting some pleasant old guy in a bar. I thought, my God, am I dreaming this, or what's going on?"

Corky then went back to sleep. The next morning at breakfast, he found out it wasn't a dream. "I did not bring this up, someone else did," Corky said. "She says, 'Do you guys have a ghost here?' When the owner said, 'Yes,' my wife and I looked at each other and couldn't believe it. That's my story and I'm stickin' with it."

They Bring Illness and Death

Dan and Carla's son John died one day, and they blame it on the Hat Man. "Our son at about 14 years said he saw dark Shadow silhouettes of figures, and they all wore tall hats," Carla said. "I never heard of such and dismissed it at first. He'd seen them often in our home, and after seeing a show, I looked it up on the computer and saw that there was others who reported this."

After John began regularly seeing these Shadow Figures, he became ill. "My son developed a virus that attacked his heart and gave him myocarditis [inflammation of the heart muscle]," Carla said. And in the hospital, John died. "His heart stopped four times as the heart surgeon attempted to install a heart bypass machine to his heart through his open chest," she said, but each time doctors were able to revive the boy. "He developed many life-threatening [illnesses], and they gave him 10 percent chance to live."

John suffered kidney failure and eventually lost both feet. John's heart and kidneys now work fine and he walks with prosthetic feet, but Carla blames his brush with death on the Shadow People with tall hats. "The Shadow People displayed themselves to him for a solid year before this virus attacked his heart," Carla said. "After two and a half months in ICU and recovery and finally coming home, he's seen a Shadow Person one more time and has not seen them since."

John is now 19 years old.

One of the Cursed

The paranormal seems to follow certain people. Are they blessed, cursed, or just unlucky? Mary Vincent of Kingston, Ontario, is one of these people, one of the unlucky or one of the cursed. Mary, at the time 17, was staying with her brother, when she realized that something in his house wasn't right.

"I was sleeping in a loft-type bedroom," she said. "I woke suddenly one night with the immediate knowledge I wasn't alone."

Sitting at the side of her bed, staring at her, was a man. "He just sat very still and the darkness of the room wouldn't allow me to see his face," she said. "It seemed as if he had a hat on. I was totally terrified. I tried to move but found I couldn't. I couldn't even turn my head away."

From her bed, she tried to scream for help, but could only manage a whisper. Then, as quickly as she'd noticed the Dark Man, he was gone. "I lay there scared and shaken," she said.

CHAPTER 13

Ouija Boards and Other Invitations to Shadows

People sometimes invite evil into their lives, willingly or unwillingly. All negative entities need is an opening and they'll slither in, and you might not even know it. Connie Stevens of Clarinda, Iowa, has been involved with the paranormal for 22 years, most recently cleansing homes and businesses of unwanted spirits. She knows that what draws evil spirits to people is a bad lifestyle.

A friend once asked her to cleanse her house and she did – many times. "The woman's husband abused her and her children and committed suicide," Connie said. "There's a lot of negative energy there. The woman keeps hanging onto her wicked husband. A problem a lot of women have is they're not altering their lifestyles to keep the sprits out. If you don't do something to change your household, they're going to come back."

Active invitations like Ouija boards and passive invitations like alcoholism, drug abuse, emotional abuse, or a gambling problem can all open your world to something sinister.

Dawn Newlan, a medium with the Ozark Paranormal Society, calls Shadow People lower-level energies, and she says, they're deceitful. "Generally, the things that come through always tell you they are a friend, a family member, a whatever," Dawn said, adding you should keep your distance from tools these entities communicate through. "Ouijas to me, and to most anyone who's been around one will tell you, they are very dangerous," she said. "When someone plays with a board they begin to open up the doorways of communication with the other side."

Negative energies come through these doorways, Dawn said. Sometimes these energies are people who were bad in life, and sometimes they are demons. "Satan has his legions," Dawn said. "If you do not know how to discern good entities from bad entities, that's when you wind up with your problems. What most people don't understand is that if you ask them a question, 'hey what is my dog's name?' [The name] is in your head. That spirit can take it out of your head and give you what you want to hear."

Dawn speaks from experience. Earlier in life, she employed one of these tools to speak with the spirit world. "I was young and stupid," she said. "Something came through and told me it was my grandma. It told me it loved me and wanted to visit me." Later the board began spelling "evil, evil, evil, evil."

"A Ouija board, until you experience it, is a fascination," Dawn said. "Your common sense tells you you really shouldn't be doing it, but your curiosity pushes you. Once it scares the hell out of you, you'll quit."

Dawn's experimentation with a Ouija board was during an emotionally stressful time as a teen and, unfortunately for her, something answered her invitation. "I actually had something evil in my house; this very large dark presence," Dawn said. "From 18 to 21, I tried hard to ignore it. The more I tried to ignore it, the more things moved in my house. People who haven't experienced that think it's make believe ... You have to deal with it [to know otherwise]."

Others, however, believe the Ouija board works, not through spirits, but through the subconscious mind of the user. "It's my preferred explanation for the phenomenon," said Ouija board user Marleigh. "One or all of the participants is moving the pointer, subconsciously. I've had it happen to me where you will ask 'what is your name' and I will think a specific name, say, 'Jason,' and without me pushing the pointer, the name Jason will be spelled out. This could explain Ouija board happenings."

Not all of the stories that follow involve Shadow People, but they are tales of invitation. These people – these victims – all opened their homes, and their lives to something negative; sometimes through Ouija boards, sometimes through spells or automatic writing.

Although the Ouija board stories dominate this chapter, the board is only one way to open dialogue with the other side. Independence, Missouri psychic Margie Kay said séances are just as dangerous. "Just like any ghost or spirit that can be called into this realm with a séance or Ouija board, Shadow People may be called in, too," she said. "That is why anyone playing with games like this that doesn't know how to protect themselves is looking for trouble."

A Few Harmless Spells

Martha moved into an old farmhouse outside St. Louis in February 2006, away from highways, concrete oceans, and close neighbors. She generally stayed alone and things were relatively quiet, until something came into her home. "Shortly after [moving in], on a whim I bought a book about spirit summoning, spells, and other bits of magic," she said. "I thought it would be fun to try a spell, so I did. Nothing life altering, something cute and mild, although it escapes me what I was trying to do at the time."

Casting the first spell roused her curiosity further, so she tried more. That's when her trouble began. "I have always had a mild interest in the occult and also enjoy a good scare now and again," she said. "But I am beginning to wonder if I might not have created some problems for myself unintentionally."

Martha may have invited negative entities into her home. According to *Disciple To Magic* by Rev. Lucian Agrippa Melampus Paul, spells and rituals "open the spiritual doors to powers and forces unseen;" doors that may best remain closed.

As the spells increased, Shadows began appearing to Martha. "It seemed the more I did, the more I began to see these Shadow People," Martha said. "At first it was just out of the corner of my eye and only for a fleeting few seconds." But the Shadows moved in and made themselves at home.

Martha stopped casting spells, but the Shadows have not left her. "They continued to progress, however, to a point where they were no longer just out of the corner of my eye, and while they wouldn't sit down and have a cup of coffee, they seemed to linger," she said. "I have a feeling both my cat and my dog see them even better than I do, as they will throw fits for no reason even in broad daylight."

The back door to Martha's home started opening on its own, straight razor blades have began appearing in odd places around her house, and the Shadows have become bolder. "I'm not just seeing Shadow People anymore; I'm seeing actual things with color and features. It is rare, but it does happen," she said. "I'm also beginning to hear things."

Martha's heard her name screamed in the house at night while sleeping, and during the day when she's fully awake. "I don't have close neighbors, so it's not just ambient noise," she said. "I've also heard music. It's pretty faint, but if I concentrate I can hear the words."

Martha hasn't dealt with it. The visitations continue, and she's beginning to doubt her sanity. "Is it really real?" Martha asked. "I'm really worried that I might be becoming a schizophrenic."

Or maybe she's just the host of a houseguest she

didn't intend to invite.

The Shadow in the Window

A plastic triangle skittered across the surface of a game board. A group of preteen girls, including Inez Pace of St. Louis, didn't believe anything supernatural had moved the piece because, after all, the Ouija board was a toy. "Early in my teenage years, my friends and I would often play with the Ouija board when we would have slee-povers," Inez said. "We would ask harmless questions as to how many children we'd have, who we'd marry, etc." Nothing really out of the ordinary happened to the girls during their play sessions, "and certainly nothing too scary," Inez said. The friends eventually outgrew their interest in Ouija boards, until the spring semester of 1983 while Inez attended Southeast Missouri State University in Cape Girardeau.

"One boring night, my dorm mates and I decided to use the common room's Ouija board," Inez said. "At first it seemed harmless enough. We'd ask silly questions and our spirit named Sarah would answer us." Inez and her friends were quickly entrapped by the Ouija, feeling "compelled to use the board as often as possible."

Then a friend named Tracy from another floor attended a Ouija session, and their harmless play turned sinister. "We started asking Sarah how she died, how old she was when she died, and finally what she looked like," Inez said. Sarah told the coeds she died at 23 when she was hit by a runaway horse and carriage.

But Sarah's answer to the final question sent the girls running. "When we asked Sarah what she looked like, she spelled out 'like Tracy only different eyes,'" Inez said. One young woman in the group asked Sarah to show them. "Tracy was a redhead with green eyes," Inez said. "Sarah spelled out for us to look at Tracy and instantly her eyes turned blue and her facial features became sharper."

Tracy screamed and said an electrical current had run through her body. "We all became excited and told Tracy what happened," Inez said. "Of course, she wanted to see it, too." Sarah spelled out for Tracy to take a mirror and look in the window behind her. As Tracy looked into the mirror, she saw someone dark and ominous standing in the room's window – a window that looked over a tree-less courtyard from three floors up.

"We looked and saw what appeared to be a head looking in at us," Inez said. "We asked the spirit, 'are you Sarah?' It went to 'no,' so we asked, 'who are you?'" The girls didn't wait for the entity's entire response. "It started to spell S-A-T-A...that was enough for me," Inez said. "I knocked the center piece off of the board and told everyone to go to their rooms. We were pretty frightened – the [Shadow Figure in the window] did not look like a lady at all."

As Inez struck the center piece off the board, the room grew cold enough the students saw their breath. They ran from Inez's room to another girl's room and began praying. "We were so frightened that none of us could sleep; we held vigil that evening to make sure nothing was going on in my room," Inez said. "Around 2:30 a.m., we decided to get a snack from the vending machine and as we walked by my door, the alarm clock went off. It had been set for 6:30 a.m."

One of the girls entered Inez's room to shut off the alarm and found the windows thrown open and sheets pulled off the beds. "As she bent down to turn off the alarm, the two necklaces she was wearing became entwined and started to choke her," Inez said. "When she got to the hallway, she removed her necklaces and noticed that the cross had been moved from one chain to the other. That was enough for us."

When the sun rose, the girls went to the Catholic house on campus and told the priest what had happened.

"He came to my room that day and blessed it with holy water," Inez said. "He also removed the board from the dorm and burned it. We got a stern lecture that as Catholics we should know better than to use something like that."

Inez graduated from Southeast Missouri State University with a degree in communications and theater in 1987. But she didn't live in that dorm room for much of that time. "It took me a while to get the courage to return to my room to sleep, and even then I always had someone stay in the room with me," Inez said. "The following year I requested a different dorm to reside in."

George, the Shadow Man

Shane Turnbeaugh, a psychic from a long line of psychics, grew up in southeast Missouri and has known Shadow People since he was a young man. He once called one into his life. "George, the Hat Man," he said. "I still encounter him to this day. Though I'm sure there must be many Hat Men, the one I'm speaking of now is somewhat special to me."

Frustrated by a stumbling point in his psychic education, a 19-year-old Shane had begun experimenting with a Ouija board. "I was eager to discover as much of the psychic realm that my mentors didn't seem to want to teach me," he said. "So I took out a Ouija Board. It took a few tries but eventually something came through. It scared the hell out of me."

As Shane sat before the board, a strange feeling crawled across him. "Every hair on the back of my neck stood straight up as the board spelled out, 'Can you feel me now?'" Shane said. "At that point I pushed the board away but it was too late."

George – later named by Shane's mother – slowly began showing itself to Shane.

"At first he was very confrontational," Shane said.

"Several days after the event I woke up in the middle of the night, got up to turn on the light in my bedroom and there he was." A Hat Man.

Shane moved toward the light, his body responding slowly to his mind's commands. "It felt like I was trying to walk against a very strong wind, and although the struggle seemed to last forever, I'm sure it was only three or four minutes," he said. "But that is a long time to fight with a Shadow to turn on your bedroom light."

Shane's Shadow remained in his mother's house – it's still there – but after a time it became "playful and mischievous," opening and shutting bedroom doors, turning Shane's television set on and off. "One night my best friend Kristie sat for 20 minutes and she would also turn my television on and he would turn it back off again," Shane said. "She could not see him, but I could."

George would turn up the volume on his television while everyone in the house was asleep. Shane feels it just wanted attention. "He seemed to feed off the attention he was given," he said. "The more attention he was given, the bolder he got. I actually got used to him being around, and I think on a couple of occasions he actually protected me from a darker entity that had followed me home from a psychic fair I had worked. Although, I suspect that more than protecting me, he was protecting his turf."

Too Close to the Spirit World

Mary Vincent of Kingston, Ontario, has been haunted by Shadow People since she was 17. Although the nature of the Shadows she first saw in her brother's bedroom remains a mystery to her, Mary wonders if she somehow invited something evil into her life. "As a young mother I started doing the Ouija board with a close friend," she said. "The more time we spent on it, the more depth the messages seemed to have."

One message was from her friend Milly's mother,

who had recently died. "She told us some personal stuff that we did not know about money left to an alienated brother," she said. The entity told Mary's friend not to fight the will, which, unbeknownst to Mary, Milly and her sister were planning to do.

Was the entity Milly's mother? According to people well versed in the Ouija board, no, the entity was demonic. But it was convincing, even down to spelling "mom," "mum," just like Milly's British mother would. Then Mary's Ouija board experiences escalated.

A group at a military camp asked her and Milly to hold a Ouija session at the base. "I knew some but not all of the people," Mary said. "We explained to them this was just for fun and we were in no way psychics."

After what Mary calls "fluff," the Ouija became alive, the planchette forcing itself across the board. "It finally spelled out a name I had never heard of," Mary said. "When I asked if anyone recognized the name, a woman – a German wife of a Canadian soldier – said it was her sister's name."

Then Mary started to feel "terrible." "I felt ill, panicky, and dark," she said. "There was no better word than 'dark' for my feelings. I told the woman that I wasn't getting a specific message just a terrible feeling. I felt angry, confused and totally unstable. She told me her sister had committed suicide."

This frightened Mary. "I realized that I was getting too close to the spirit side and, in this case, it wasn't a good feeling," she said. "I have never sat at the Ouija board since."

But she couldn't stay away from the paranormal. Curious about automatic writing, she allowed something unseen to write with her hand. "I twice tried automatic writing," she said. "The first time, when the pen started to move, I got scared, being alone, and threw the pen."

But that didn't stop her from attempting to contact the spirit world again. "The second time I kept my head averted but let the pen write," she said. "When I looked at it, I saw various words that didn't mean anything but in the last place it said 'Mary Elizabeth, it's Grandma Hogeboom.'"

The handwriting of the last five words wasn't Mary's. "I took the paper to my mother and she pulled out an old card my grandmother had once sent her," she said. "The handwriting was identical. Absolutely identical. My mother flipped out."

Did Mary channel her grandmother, or did something evil write with her hand?

I Know What I Saw

On May 7, 2007, John Prato was awakened by banging noises from the room above his. "After that, I saw something almost unbelievable and captured it with my camcorder," he said. "I was sitting down on my chair adjusting my camcorder, waiting to hear more banging sounds, and then all of a sudden a dark Shadow moved very fast and it passed right by me. It scared the heck out of me."

Prato didn't realize what happened until he looked at the video. "I watched it...and saw it again with my own eyes," he said. "I watched it one more time [and] when I got near that part, I paused it and then I watched it frame-by-frame and saw this large dark Shadow. It was the most frightening thing I've ever seen."

The Shadow Man that had just walked through Prato's room was about ten feet tall and four feet wide. "Just by looking at it, you could tell it's nonhuman," he said.

But there was something more to the video – as the Shadow Man walked past him, the light in the room grew dim. Prato is sure he knows where the Shadow man came from. "It came from my homemade Ouija board that I used on May 8, 2006," he said. "After I used my Ouija board, I started hearing loud banging sounds on the wall the next day, and it's the same wall where the large dark Shadow came from. It's been here ever since." Prato posted the video of his Shadow Man on YouTube. Watch it and judge for yourself.

We've Met in Real Life

A Shadow Man roams Jennifer's home. It walks around her bedroom watching her, and sometimes it speaks. "I've been dealing with a Shadow Man for a while now," Jennifer said. "I'll see a man walking around in my room. When I'm laying down, I can feel it touching me and playing with my hair as well as stroking my cheek."

As Jennifer lies helpless under its touch, the Shadow Man sometimes speaks to her. "I heard it call my name a few times and say things like 'I love you,' and 'I'll never let you go,'" she said. Terrified of this intruder, she tried to capture its image – and she did.

"One night I left my camera on and put it on Record. I was hoping to see something in the camera," she said. "To my surprise it looked like a real man. He had curly brown hair, blue eyes, and looked to be in his late 20s/ early 30s."

Then Jennifer bought a Ouija board and found her obsessive Shadow Man claimed to be a living, breathing stalker. "It had told me it was a real person and that he was astral-projecting," she said. "I started to ask this being things like, 'how long have you been watching me?'"

The planchette spelled out "Three years."

"How did you find me?"

"I felt your energy level," it replied.

"Have we met in real life?" Jennifer asked.

"Yes," the entity wrote.

Then Jennifer challenged her Shadow stalker. "Why don't you ever come talk to me face-to-face in real life?" she asked.

The entity's last words to her were, "I'm shy."

After that he refused to answer her questions. Jennifer may have unwittingly attracted some evil entity into her life, but her Shadow Man's claim leaves her wondering, "What if some of these Shadow People are real people who are astral-projecting?" Or, was this just one of these lower-level energies pulling off a grand deception?

CHAPTER 14

Other Explanations

Are these Shadow People inter-dimensional travelers? Extraterrestrials? Demons? The product of sleep paralysis? Chemical imbalances in the brain? Or are they something else? Many people who have seen these black Shadows lurking in the once-friendly corners of their bedroom are certain that Shadow People are something else.

Becky saw the Shadow Man as a child, but she doesn't know what it was. "In the apartment where I spent most of my childhood there was a Shadow Man that would walk back and forth in the hallway," she said. "At first I was terrified, but eventually I got used to him. He had really negative energy."

But unlike most reports of Shadow People with negative energy, Becky said the feeling was different than something feeding off fear. It was "more depression," she said, "less anger."

Protective Spirits

The girl gripped the sheets with shaky little hands as the Shadow Person walked toward her bed. Patti Starr, a psychic who now teaches ghost hunting classes in Lexington, Kentucky, was terrified of the giant, Shadow Man.

"A lot of times they're big," she said. "They always appeared at night when I had gotten in bed. A lot of times they sat in bed with me, and a lot of times they'd tease me. They'd pull my covers and that would terrify me."

But later, after years of the horror of watching these entities walk through her room and feel the weight of their bodies as they sat upon her bed, she realized she shouldn't fear these Shadows. "I found it was a protective situation," she said. Starr grew up with a psychologically abusive mother, and the Shadow Man would appear to her in times of trouble.

"A lot of times the Shadow Person appeared in my bedroom," she said. "He still appears today. Usually when I'm stressed, but it's okay."

Starr's mother, an evangelical Christian, never believed her young daughter's cries of terror as the Shadow Man sat on her bed, but at the end, she understood what her daughter had lived through. "[The Shadow Man] came to me while my mother was dying," she said. "Before she died she saw the Shadow Person and described him. I said, 'that's the Shadow Person I've seen all my life.'"

As a psychic, Starr studies colors and auras, and thinks the color black explains the true nature of these Shadow People. "Most often, Shadow People are dark. The color black is a protection color. When you want to banish an evil spirit, you use a black candle because a candle protects you."

Starr has captured pictures of black orbs and mists she feels very comfortable with. "I think they are for comfort and support," she said. "Even though you don't understand that energy, that energy is there. There's a comfort, or otherwise you'd feel a lot worse."

Astral Travelers

The Shadows sat across one side of a semi-circle table, cloaked, piercing holes for eyes fixed on a crowd of people. Dawn Sevier of Sparta, Tennessee, who has been haunted by Shadow People, thought this was a dream – but it felt so real. "There was more than one, there were nine," she said. "Each one was allowing their eyes to be seen. All the eyes were black, the blackest black I've ever seen, and they were looking out on a crowd of people who were there to voice concerns."

Dreaming, Dawn walked to the table and looked at each of nine shadows, one by one. "None acknowledged that I was standing in front of them observing them," she said. "In my dream, I had no fear at all. After I reached the last Shadow, two people grabbed me and carried me through the crowd and put me into the back of a white limousine. I awoke feeling disturbed and have never forgotten this dream."

Many parapsychologists consider dreams – especially lucid dreams, dreams that seem too real to be just dreams – to be a form of astral projection. You're consciously aware during the dream and can control your actions while your soul travels outside your body – as can the very real entities you may encounter there. Dawn's soul may have stood before that council of nine, but she doesn't know who they were judging, or who in the white limousine stepped in to save her.

Online poster Treacle doesn't consider these occurrences dreams. Treacle leaves his body when he sleeps, sometimes intentionally, sometimes not. But when he began trying to astral travel, Treacle started seeing a Shadow Person. "I eventually got around to talking to it after having seen it a number of times," he said. "I asked it what it was, and it said 'I'm a Lackey.' Aside from the common use of the word, I have no idea what that means."

Treacle feels no fear when he sees Lackey out of the corner of his eye, but he's still cautious. "It wasn't scary," he said. "I really felt that it was somewhat playful and shy, but not really dangerous. I could never see it head-on. This was, by the way, during waking life."

But when Treacle sleeps, things change. "Consider what happened to me tonight [July 5, 2008]," he said. "I was sleeping in front of my computer, and I woke to find that my consciousness was floating a few inches above my physical body. I was then spun around maybe about halfway and pulled across the room by some unknown force."

Was that force Lackey? Maybe. Treacle never saw what grabbed his astral form. "This sort of thing doesn't really freak me out, but it does make me feel like getting back in my body and waking it up rather than deciding to go exploring," he said. "It's just not a pleasant way to be woken up to that world. However, that's just the way it sometimes happens, so I am willing to accept that I will sometimes deal with some weird stuff."

Treacle is an admitted novice to astral travel, experiencing paralysis and an overwhelming urge to return to his body, but when his experience will allow him to travel in time and space, maybe he'll meet Lackey along the road, or maybe Treacle will become another Shadow Person story for others who happen to catch a glimpse of Treacle's astral form.

Shadow People May Not Be Evil

Ryan Straub of Centralia, Missouri, founder of the paranormal research group Tir Firnath, has seen Shadow People – and other things – since he was a teenager. "I see things frequently," he said. "I have been seeing spirits since a car wreck at age 16."

Straub, now 24, investigates the paranormal in Missouri and surrounding states, and in some of those investigations he's encountered Shadow People. "I was doing a walk-through at an abandoned nursing home," he said, where broken windows stare at visitors to this four-story building infested with ghostly legends. "Stories have been told about the location and I was on a mission to verify the late night howling, slamming doors and windows, phantom patients and pets, and lights and plumbing turning on and off" although no electricity has been in the building for at least 10 years, he said.

Straub walked through the building with a disposable camera and shot pictures arbitrarily. "When I came across the basement of the building I came across an old wheelchair, took a picture and went on with the walkthrough," Straub said. "Upon looking at the developed pictures I came across various orbs and mist. When I came to the wheelchair picture, there was a phantom greyhound sitting in it. This I found very interesting and upon closer examinations of the photo noticed several Shadow People in the background."

Shadows in the background. That's where these entities – no matter what they are – seem to operate. But Straub said just because Shadow People operate in the dark doesn't mean they're bad. "A lot of reasons people say they're demons is they're associating black with evil," he said. "Why can't it be positive or even neutral? People aren't seeing them as a warning, but as a cause of the problem."

One person, Straub said, is going to see a Shadow Person as a helpful omen and another is going to see it as threatening. "People claim to see guardian angels and demons," he said. "But [Shadow People] have to be some sort of higher power. Maybe this is as high as a human being can be without being an angel or demon."

Although Straub doesn't claim to know what Shadow People are, through research in Wiccan, Native American, and Old World pagan traditions, he has some ideas. "What these things could be are spirits or messengers or ancestors from the spiritual realm with more energy than ghosts so they're not translucent. They come forth as a Shadow."

Whatever Shadow People are, Straub said they seem to be territorial and may be a product of our own conscious energies. "We have no real evidence stating what they are," Straub said. "People see them, people are affected by them. There's no true evidence of them except people photograph them once in a while. What if these things are solely created because they are thought to exist?"

ETs

Most explanations of Shadow People are grounded in psychology or the spirit world, but some believe there is a much more otherworldly explanation – extraterrestrials. Gil McDonald, Sr., a retired security guard from the federal penitentiary in Jefferson City, Missouri, has seen Shadow Beings at the prison; things he's sure are not from our planet. "I saw a lot of those. I think they're from out of the cosmos," he said. "Some of them look like humans except they're gray; like they're drawn in pencil or something. Several times I have seen them walk directly through a solid object."

Although McDonald initially kept quiet about the entities, he decided to talk about his encounters after these Shadow Beings began following him. "It's like they go home with you," he said. "I don't really know what they're doing." But whatever the entities' purpose, Gil said he doesn't think it's benevolent. He said he's seen evidence we may be lunch. "It makes me think that we're not on the top of the food chain," he said. "It looks like they're using humans. I think they take some people and don't bring them back. We should not trust them."

"From the Shadows" poster Truthseeker believes people are experiencing extraterrestrials and calling them Shadow People – she knows because she's been abducted. "They were what I refer to as aliens...I call them aliens because that's what makes the most sense to me," Truthseeker said. "They're not human, and presumably not from this Earth, and seem to be interested in doing 'experiments' on people."

Truthseeker can't remember the number of her abduction experiences, or remember everything that happened during them, but her last encounter was in the mid

1990s. "Why they would allow me to remember the last one pretty well but only small fragments of the previous ones, I'm not sure," she said. They were "terrifying things in every way. Terrifying is an understatement. There is not a word in the English language that can adequately describe the terror and fear of these experiences. I just hope they are 'done' with me."

Reptilian ETs

Reptilian extraterrestrials – thought by some to be as the biblical serpent in Genesis and the toads mentioned in Revelation – have been popular villains in science fiction for decades. Some UFOlogists believe that these Reptilians, if they exist, can change their shape to look identical to humans and hold major positions in world government. The 1983 TV miniseries *V* has these shape-shifting Reptilian aliens taking over humanity. But many ancient cultures – such as the Mayans, the Neolithic Europeans, and the Japanese – all have Reptilian humanoids as part of their mythology.

Can these Reptilians correspond with Shadow People? Michael Lynch, Ph.D. is convinced they do. "What I will tell you will be unbelievable," he said. "The first kind is Reptilian, wearing a black-hooded robe." Lynch said this Reptilian entity can move slightly out of sync with our reality, which creates the two-dimensional Shadow most often reported. "But when the Reptilian slows down, he becomes more visible."

"From the Shadows" reader John sees these Reptilian Shadow People in his dreams. "I had a dream about one in a hood only it was black and it had a snake head," he said. "It was a witch and sending evil spirits around." The spirits flew from the whirling current of a tornado that dominated his dream.

"After I began to wake up I opened my eyes and kin-da saw it standing at the end of the bed with that fear feeling," he said. "And then it was gone."

That fear dominates these dream encounters, as if the Shadow People are feeding off the terror they evoke. "In another dream, it was all black, and hovering amidst a portal with what looked like a staff," John said. "It was trying to crush me with intense fear, and I tried to call out for Jesus, but couldn't. So I had to believe with my heart, and light came out and either sent it away or destroyed it. I woke up feeling better than I had in a long, long time."

Metaphysical author Jack Allis said the malevolent extraterrestrial hypothesis is not out of the question. "As far as what's going on on the planet Earth, I believe it's pretty obvious that the dark side has been in control of this dimension for at least 6,000 years," he said. "And it's in control of this planet for the benefit of their food."

Allis said these extraterrestrials have been involved with humanity for "a very, very long time," interbreeding with humans to gain control of the ruling factions of this planet and promoting violence because the Reptilians feed on the fear violence brings. "There are those who believe these genetic ET hybrids are actually behind the scenes powers that are ruling the world," Allis said. "They feed upon human fear, that's why they endeavored to create the kind of earth they created."

Wars, poverty, famine, Allis said, are all products these entities draw energy from. "They feed upon all negative human emotions. Fear, anger, hostility. Those kind of negative emotions are created by these entities," he said. "As far as the existence of malevolent ETs, I'm absolutely convinced."

After an encounter with these beings, Danny Smith is certain Lynch and Allis are correct – Shadow People are these Reptilian extraterrestrials – and he's terrified. "I saw one when I was young," Danny said. "He told me that they can bend the color spectrum so that we can't see them. They have six webbed fingers and a sleek near-ly snakelike skin texture. He held his hand up to show me."

But, although this Reptilian Shadow Person spoke with Danny, he was angry Danny had seen him. "He said he was going to kill me," Danny said. "But I told him I was just a little kid and nobody would ever believe me."

Fear engulfing him, Danny prayed to Jesus to send the creature home, and it was dragged from his room. "It was suddenly encased in a strange bubble, and it grew smaller and smaller and began to fade," Danny said. "It yelled at me that it was over 900 years old and that it would only have to wait in Hell for 42 years before it could come back and kill me for what I'd done. That was 42 years ago."

Although Lynch believes in the existence of Reptilian ETs that appear as Shadows, he said there are also Shadow People who come from the spirit realm. "Most people will say spiritual and then there are some that will say alien," Lynch said. "I think that it is about 50/50 myself."

A Little Bit of Everything

A metallic noise rang through a hallway in the West Virginia Penitentiary in Moundsville, West Virginia, stopping Polly Gear, who had just walked through the hall. Gear and her group, Mountaineer Ghosts Paranormal Investigators, were investigating the empty structure on May 7, 2004; she heard the noise at about 1:30 a.m.

"I turn and go back to the small hallway that I had just walked through and I clicked on my flashlight to check the area," she said. "As soon as my light came on, I saw this black human-shaped Shadow walking toward me."

But the Shadow – that worked its way to within 10 feet of Gear – wasn't looking at her, it was looking out a large window as it worked its way down the hall. "This sounds off the wall, but its movements as it was walking – before it saw me – were somewhat animated," Gear said. The Shadow Person was a "perfect" human shape with no facial features and made no sound.

Then it saw her. Gear turned her flashlight on the Shadow figure and it panicked. "I put my light directly on it and it took a second or two for this thing to notice it had light on its body," she said. "As it noticed this light, it brought its arm up some to look at the light shinning on it, then immediately it started looking in my direction."

When it saw Gear, it dashed behind a door. "It looked 3-D as it was face-on to me, but as it turned to the side to dash behind the door facing, it was a very thin 2-D thing, almost like a peel-off sticker," she said. "Something deep in me told me to start backing off or it would disappear."

Gear started walking backward down the hallway, directing her flashlight to the floor. She took out a digital camera to take a picture of the spot where the Shadow Person had gone, but when she turned it on, the camera chimed, and the Shadow Man came back. "I simply held out the camera and took one snapshot toward where I last saw the Shadow Person behind the doorway," Gear said. "Apparently [the] musical jingle sound … made the entity step out from the doorway to look at me."

She couldn't see the Shadow Person until she lightened the photograph. "I nearly missed the opportunity, that is how dark it was in there, I couldn't see the doorway either," she said. "As I snapped the pic, I saw it standing there looking at me, then it was instantly gone. I ran back to where it had been, checked the whole area – no one or nothing was there."

Gear and her team took various measurements of the area and observed it under light, but nothing seemed out of the ordinary. "The one thing that interested me most was how it looked at its own arm with light from my flashlight on it," Gear said. "Like it didn't like the light, or was afraid of it. I've often wondered if light destroyed or damaged it or was it just terrified of light? I don't know what the camera flash has done to it if anything."

Unlike many Shadow People encounters, Gear felt nothing negative from her Shadow Person. "As a matter of fact, I think it was afraid of me, or possibly afraid of the light I had," she said. Because of its behavior, Gear believes this entity was a ghost. "It seemed to be a guard on his daily rounds, or an inmate walking through from the cafeteria," she said. "This Shadow Person was one of the most interesting paranormal encounters I've ever had as a paranormal investigator."

Although Gear feels this encounter was with a ghost, she's open to other explanations. "Could they be more than one type?" she said. "I don't know what they are factually, but I do have an opinion from the way the one I was within 10 feet of acted – before and after it saw me. I lean toward this one being the shell that was left of a person that was killed in an unspeakable way."

The figure appeared like a "black void of static" inside the shape of a man. "I do believe Shadow People are more than one type, but I don't feel they are demons," she said. "There was absolutely no negativity about them."

Gear's second Shadow People encounter led her to quite a different explanation. The Mountaineer Ghosts Paranormal group was asked to investigate an old house for sale in St. Clairsville, Ohio. Gear sat on the floor in the bare house, under a window in a second-story bedroom, the faint glow of a streetlight the only light gently bathing the room and illuminating the bedroom door she faced.

"I saw an extremely black Shadow, head and shoulders, in the light reflecting on the bedroom door, raise straight up from the bottom of the window's shadow, stay there for three seconds, and then glide straight back down toward the bottom of the window sill," she said. The Shadow's head seemed overly large for the long, skinny neck and thin shoulders.

A group member yelled out "did you see that?" Gear said yes, "but WTF was it?" Then they started laughing. "It was so comical how this thing showed itself," Gear said. "It seemed mechanical in the movement. It didn't shake, or wobble, or change shape. It was a perfectly smooth glide up and down."

Thinking someone had possibly climbed up to the window to peek in, Gear shot up and looked out the window. "There is no way anyone could have done what I thought," she said. "They would have had to be 15 feet tall. It seemed that whatever it was was having fun with us."

The next morning, Gear remembers something odd about the Shadow in the window. "I called the girl that saw it too and said, 'did you notice this thing have any hair?'" she said. "She thinks and says, 'no, no it didn't.'"

The women also remembered the entity had no ears and were hesitant to say what they both were thinking. "At the time and throughout that night we never noticed this, only later the next day," she said. "So from the size of the head, no hair or ears, and its comical attitude has lead me to go along the lines of this one being more of the alien type. I can't even believe that I am saying it, but I am."

Ghost or aliens, Gear is convinced there are many different types of Shadow entities. "They could be ghosts, they could be aliens," she said. "And I feel that aliens are inter-dimensional entities. But I only came to this conclusion from my experiences of watching them. There was nothing scientific there to make either of the experiences happen."

Or all these suggestions could be connected. Patrick Heron, author of *Nephilim and the Pyramid of the Apocalypse*, is convinced Shadow People, ghosts, and space aliens are one in the same. "I am a Bible man and I take my direction from its truths," Heron said. "I delve into demons and fallen angels... That's who these ghosts are, either demons or spirits which are fallen angels. Absolutely, no doubt about it. Folks have different names for things but they are all the same entities. Aliens equal ETs equal fallen angels equal evil spirits equal the Nephilim."

Shadow People could be anything. According to longtime paranormal researcher and author Brad Steiger, author of *Shadow World*, "In the field of the paranormal, there are no experts. We're all learning."

CHAPTER 15

Kaci's Cry for Help

I am often contacted by people who are curious, angry, or afraid of something strange happening in their lives. If I can, I give them advice. If I can't, I point them in directions where they can find answers on their own. Or I forward them to experts who can help them better than me.

Then, one day I heard from Kaci, someone who sees things in the dark recesses of everyday life most people can't see. This case interested me not just because of Kaci's claims of the paranormal, but because she wasn't looking for anything other than a way to help people preyed upon by Shadow People.

May 7, 2008, 9:36 p.m. (posted on From-the-Shadows.blog-spot.com): "My name is Kaci. Me and my friends see the Shadow People. We each have special gifts. My gifts are seeing the dead, seeing the future, and seeing the Shadow People. For some reason the Shadow People wish to harm me and my friends. We're looking for others like us with our abilities. We aren't crazy, we don't need mental help. We need answers. If you have abilities like ours please contact me…You're not alone. We can help you control your gift. I'm not a fake. Please contact me if you're one of us.

May 8, 2008, 10:20 p.m. (e-mail to me): The five of us try to hide our abilities because we don't want to seem like freaks or get put away because of the things we see. We are looking for answers and others like us. We want to help them. The Shadow People we encounter are harmful. I was driving home one night and a Shade [Shadow Person] reached over and tried to jerk the steering wheel. I almost lost control. Today I saw my uncle who died when I was in the second grade. He watches over me and since then I have been seeing the dead. The dead, Shades, and the future are not things you wanna mess with. I won't tell you anymore about us because there are things even you are not meant to know about, at least not yet. If there is a way you can help us find others like us with our abilities you would really be helping us.

May 11, 2008, 2:35 p.m. (email): Jason, I need your help to get my message out to people. I get emails from people telling me who they are and what they can do but we are looking for more people. My visions can only show me so much. They help me point out the fakes but that doesn't leave us with many people. They are laughing at us but we're trying to help people. Those who leave you comments, some of them are scared. We can help them block the images. For a while I did it. Please help us find our friends.

May 11, 2008, 2:52 p.m. (posted on From-the-Shadows.blog-spot.com): Guys, listen I need you to read my comments. We are searching for others like us. We have some answers that I know you guys are looking for. The five of us will help you. Please contact me…

May 11, 2008, 11:17 p.m. (email): There isn't a whole lot I can tell you because there are certain things you're not suppose to know about yet. The five of us have been a well-kept secret for a long time. We are normal like everyone else. I know that they are scared. When I came into my powers, I was so scared I didn't know what to do. I was seeing dead people and having them all come to me saying they don't know they are dead. FYI, don't talk to the dead. We aren't sure who are good and who are bad. One follows me frequently and he appears to be neither living nor dead. We just ignore him. There is one thing we all share, we are all blessed with incredible luck, it protects us, it helps us, and it keeps us safe. We aren't positive where our luck comes from but I believe it's a pentagram. I was on a road one day and I didn't see a wall I was coming straight at and I just barely escaped. A pentagram was drawn on the wall. Since then I keep one drawn on the palm of my hand and it changes traffic lights for me, sometimes protects me from Shades and it gives us power. We will help anyone that comes to us. I can help them block their images. We'll help anyway we can. We need help finding others like us. Thanks for all the help, Jason. You're really saving a lot of people.

May 14, 2008, 1:27 p.m. (email): Jason, I don't know what you did, but people are starting to come to us. We are really starting to help people. Our powers help separate the fakes from the real people. Slowly they are starting to join our team. Thank you so much.

May 21, 2008, 7:51 p.m. (email): Teens, kids, and parents are all sending us e-mails. We're really making a difference. Some have agreed to join us.

May 21, 2008, 8:20 p.m. (email, in response to questions):
1) My powers are visions, Shades, and the dead. I realized I had them the day I saw a Shade attack my friend and I had a vision in my car foreseeing my friend's accident (she was okay, it was a minor accident but still scary).
2) My powers are limited by rules and taboos. If I break one I lose my powers. That also goes for my team because my one friend just recently ascended into her powers. The universe is personal gain. I only see what is needed to be seen. I cannot change history but others can. I cannot interfere.

3) I use them to foresee who are the fakes. Who is using us, who is laughing at us. I use my own experiences to help their own powers.

4) Our safety is the most important thing. We're not about to let people put us away because of what we think. Others would think we're crazy. Hell, I think I'm crazy, but you know we just manage as is. We're as normal as anyone else. And no one knows about our powers until we are absolutely sure.

5) There are five of us including myself. My closest friend just ascended and has my powers. I believe two more are due to ascend soon.

6) The other side we don't talk to. Those who have died and still remain here have not crossed over. They try to get my attention, but until I know more about them, we don't speak. Spirits and the dead are two different things. My uncle is a spirit. He came to me once. They don't speak of where they go, only that they are okay and tell me not to worry.

7) Shades have chased us for months. They tried to hit my car. They have gotten into our heads and tried to get rid of us. Visions get scarier and the dead just wander completely lost. It's sad. There isn't a whole lot we can do, but every day I uncover new information and I develop my powers as much as possible. Today, I uncovered more troublesome information, but my team and I must confirm the information before we just dismiss it.

8) A Shade once reached his hand into my car and grabbed my steering wheel. He tried to jerk my car. I screamed at him to back off before he would regret it and he was gone. He was lucky, not me. We are all blessed with luck. That's what protects us. The source of our luck we have yet to find out yet but I believe it is the pentagram since there are 5 points and 5 of us.

9) Shades are evil. We don't know what they want, but I know that they are after us, and others like us, and that is why we are coming together.

10) Don't do anything reckless because that's what they want. That means no speeding in cars, and just be careful in what you do because they look for that stuff to make something go wrong. And I wouldn't stay out in the dark alone.

11) I'm sorry, but for the protection of my team I cannot tell you where we operate. We are a well-kept secret and I can't risk complete exposure. People are still turning to us and we are more than happy to help them. My team and I think it was a good idea to find others. Oh, gotta go. I think a Shade just got in my house and I know he doesn't want to mess with me.

May 22, 2008, 1:41 p.m. (email): I caught the Shade. They have been stalking us like crazy lately so either a new enemy is in town or something is going on and they are monitoring us big time. My friends will remain anonymous that's why I haven't given you their names. You may use my name but we can't tell you anything else about where we come from that's for our own safety.

June 12, 2008, 1:07 p.m. (email): This week has been pretty intense. Actually, I just told my boyfriend what I am. He surprisingly took it well.

June 13, 2008, 3:24 p.m. (email): I feel like a celebrity. Emails are coming in left and right. The night I told my boyfriend about what I am, a Shade was watching us on his balcony. It jumped over the edge and blended in with other Shadows on the ground. I think every time I tell someone, they end up seeing what I see. Me and my friends have been attacked ever since.

June 14, 2008, 3:55 p.m. (email): Something is wrong. Shades are starting to go after children. If this is so, then something big is going down with them. I don't know what will happen now but this puts us in a tight spot.

June 23, 2008, 12:51 p.m. (email): I'm trying to save one of my members. I had a vision he was going to get kidnapped, and he never listens to anything I say. Something doesn't feel right about today. I don't know what it is, but it's just an unpleasant feeling. Maybe it has something to do with everything that's been happening the past week. More info on that later. I've got my hands full now.

June 25, 2008, 3:31 p.m. (email): I made a breakthrough. Sound, music. This may be the connection I'm looking for. I can't believe I never saw it before. When I'm in the car and I feel like I'm being watched, I put music on and I'm left alone. I think it's the sound waves or something. Last night the guys thought it would be a good idea to find some Shades near the house and test the theory. It works; they hate music. I need to look more into this. If there is a way to fight back I think I found the answers I'm looking for. – Sincerely, Kaci and the Others.

CHAPTER 16

Getting Rid of Shadows

Music may not be the only solution.

Stephanie Wentz, her mother, and stepfather moved into a quiet apartment. "We settled in and thankfully nothing occurred for over a year," she said. "In this apartment I went from thirteen to fourteen and from fourteen to fifteen without any problems."

Then new neighbors moved in – "a Hispanic family with an apparent devout faith in God." The family was polite and quiet, until the yelling started. "One day my mom told me she saw a sickly woman arriving to their apartment with her husband and thought nothing of it," she said. The family often held Bible study sessions in their apartment. "However, when my mom went into her room and laid on her bed she heard yelling coming from their apartment," Wentz said.

The master bedroom and bathroom shared a wall with the next apartment's kitchen and living room. "She said they were shouting biblical things in Spanish," Wentz said. "Since my mother is Cuban and speaks Spanish fluently, she said it sounded like an exorcism." The shouts and screams continued for about an hour, then abruptly stopped. "The woman left in a very weak state, my mom said, but didn't look as sick as she did when she arrived."

Neither Wentz nor her mother was ready for what the exorcism had thrust into their home. "The next night I was awake and getting ready for bed. I went out of my room and to the kitchen for water," Wentz said. "As I walked back, I noticed something in the hallway where our front door is. Something was standing in front of the wall that we shared with the apartment next door."

The something was tall, it's cowled head almost brushing the ceiling. "It was clearly visible and was an impossibly dark black color," she said. "The Shadow looked like it was wearing a robe or a cloak that reached its feet. I was frozen to the spot. I was terrified. It was worst level of fear I've ever felt in my whole life."

The Shadow lurched forward and began running at her. Wentz bolted, reaching her room and slamming the door behind her. "The entire time I ran that short distance of ten feet to my room I felt the Shadow right on my back – mere centimeters from touching me," she said. "I didn't sleep that night. I never left the room until morning. I was afraid the thing was waiting outside my door."

Wentz and her family are convinced the exorcism conducted by their neighbors was successful – and let loose a demon into their home.

Exorcist James Bucknam said entities like this could be demons or Shadow People – he's seen and banished both. "I have been successfully removing entities such as ghosts, poltergeists, Shadow People, and the occasional demon from people's homes for the past thirteen years," he said.

With his years of experience ridding people of whatever's haunting them, Bucknam has discovered Shadow People are nothing to be taken lightly. "Most paranormal groups and others fail to recognize the danger of dealing with these types of beings," he said. "Exposing yourself to them could lead to disruptions in your life of a negative variety."

Once these entities thrust themselves into someone's life, they tend to stay there. "I have discovered that where you find one Shadow Person, you tend to find more, very close by," Bucknam said. "They always operate in groups – never alone. Also they are negative in their orientation, and must be dealt with carefully."

An anonymous poster to the paranormal blog "From the Shadows" said a way to prevent Shadow People from entering your life is to not be negative: "Live a good life. Make the best of what you have been given. Don't hate or judge other people. Catch yourself when you are thinking negatively. Kick bad thoughts out of your mind. You must make a conscious effort to accomplish this. Remember, some of these beings are hundreds of years old. You are a young soul, no matter how old you are. These energies have been gaining strength for hundreds, sometimes thousands of years. No matter how strong you are, you may not be strong enough, and that is when to ask God for help. He promises protection, not for your physical body, but definitely for your soul. If you've given your soul to him, it is his responsibility to protect it. He will not let you down, you are a part of him."

But how do you get rid of Shadow People? Some paranormal investigators, like Alexandra Gargiulo, say you do it with prayer. "Entities can and do prey on people as they have energies far stronger than ours at times," she said. "Oftentimes they are not alone and are accompanied by 'others' that I call 'helpers' to assist in the attack. It doesn't last long, but it happens and there is nothing you can do but pray."

Prayer
From the ages of three years to fourteen years, Shadow People terrified Sandra Danville. "I had nightly visits and, in the years to come, day visits as well," she said. "I've been held down unable to move or speak in some visits, but just thinking about the Blood of Christ makes them go away."

Danville's Shadow People had green glowing eyes and increased in number with each visit to the point she could no longer count them. But she learned how to defeat them. "After the first wave of fear hits, stand strong and tell them to be gone for Christ blood is upon you and no evil can stand against this," she said. "Sometimes I still get visits, but they stand far from me for they fear now."

Pastor Harry Walther of the Church of Philadelphia-Internet and author of *The Answer – Two Raptures*, said Danville's approach is correct. "I believe these Shadow People are demons," he said. "They do attack people and flee when the name of Jesus is used – I speak from personal experience."

When demons attack, Walther said they almost always appear as Shadow People. "My dog actually barks when one is present, as they like to appear in corners," Walther said. "We cast them out in Jesus' name and they do leave. Be careful as these things are dangerous."

Prayer and Comedy

In Autumn 2006, William Kent was sitting in his living room in Plymouth, UK, watching television, when a grapefruit-sized round, dark Shadow, jumped from the floor onto the sofa next to him. "It made a sound as it jumped onto some papers next to me," he said. "I said aloud, 'What the hell was that?'"

As the words died, a featureless, black, Shadow Man appeared at the side of the sofa, bent forward slightly as if curious, then vanished. "I was frightened but I didn't feel any malicious intent," Kent said. "There was a highly electrical charge in the room for about 30 minutes afterwards. It made the fillings in my teeth tingle."

Kent later moved, and the Shadows followed him. "This time, I was plagued one night," he said. "Three times I was woken from sleep; twice by something or someone pinching me. It felt like a needle prick or a bee sting. First my wrist, then after I'd shone my torch around and told them to go away, I turned onto my side, went back to sleep and they pinched my bum."

Kent saw long, bony fingers and two mischievous child-like Shadow entities. He spent the rest of the night with the lights on, and the pinching Shadows left him alone. Kent later developed a house protection ritual he conducts every evening, and the Shadows have left him alone – so far. This is his ritual in his words:

1) Stand under or next to a strong white light. Imagine drawing the white light through your head and all the way down your spine. Go though each bone, illuminating your spine. If you get a jolt, just release it. Try and fill your spine up with light and also the space behind your spine.

2) In my mind and using my hands to channel light, visualize drawing the light from the bulb/Source of All Love/Life/ God and/or whatever Divine Goodness source works for you. With light, seal the door to your house/flat or the bottom of stairs or wherever the entrance to where you live is. Draw a circle and quarter it. I draw the light circle three times, then a vertical, then a horizontal. Think: "God, protect this place." Then I draw a light "wall" all the way tracing the wall/boundary of the house where my flat is. Any places you sense as needing extra protection, put an extra quartered circle seal there. Complete the outer perimeter of the house (if you're in a flat, do the whole house.)

Now, starting from the roof, stand and physically draw your hands up, reach up, put light at the top of the roof, and draw a ribbon of light down either side of the house, both sides, to the ground, passing under the house, meeting at the middle. Say/think: "God, protect this house. Thanks." Then I do it again, length-wise. At the apex, I put a light-seal.

Now I go into each room and say: "Okay, you folks, anyone who doesn't live here, who shouldn't be here, it's time for you to go home. Off you go, back to your own dimension." Be firm. Clap your hands if need be. Then seal the window and any stairwell windows as you do the house.

Then I seal the bed. IMPORTANT: Stand at base of bed. Cast a seal three times, totally enclosing the bed. Say: "God, protect this bed and its occupant, myself, tonight and always,

Amen. Thanks." Now loop two hoops of light around it, repeating the words. One encloses the bed lengthwise, one widthwise. Then I place another seal above the bed. Then one above my pillow and finally, I enclose the whole bed once more in a light circle.

Then move to the next room. Ask anything that shouldn't be there to go home. Seal the window. Seal anything like a loft hatch/ventilation extractor opening etc. Then relax.

And the Shadow People have left him alone. "Fortunately, since finding and doing this protection ritual, I've slept fine," Kent said. "I think it's up to all of us to affirm and strengthen our direct connection to God. That way, even if there's evil, its effect is to help us become stronger. Fight back with light, prayer, and humor. Watch comedy films and TV. Avoid depressing, violent material. Pray. Believe me – it works."

Shadows on the Walls

John Dunlap III, 22, felt lost. When he went looking for answers, he found something unexpected.

"John was having personal problems at the time and was 'soul searching' to find answers to his questions," said Ryan Straub of the mid-Missouri paranormal investigation group Tir Firnath. "He asked if I could help him in a guided meditation in order to find his answers."

While Straub placed Dunlap in a trance, "the event" happened. "I was being put under by Ryan because I needed answers to some of life's questions," Dunlap said. "As I was going into trance, I glanced above me and noticed four Shadowy figures."

These Shadow Figures remained above Dunlap during his soul search and, as he was coming out of his trance, they didn't want to let him go. "As I concluded my journey, the Shadows 'melted' from the wall and grabbed onto my foot," Dunlap said. "At this point, I got very cold and out of breath. I started getting restless. This is when

Ryan said a protection spell and threw some herbs into a lit candle. The Shadow Figure felt like it was being drug off."

As Dunlap felt the Shadow Figures release him, a glass jar containing a nearby candle shattered – and the Shadow Figure was gone. "I have seen glimpses out of the corners of my eyes and have heard whispering when no one else was around," Dunlap said. "[But] before the event I was skeptical. The event spooked me and opened me up to the paranormal."

Shadow Battle

A dark, black figure hovered over Candice's sleepless form, a foot or two over her legs and midsection. But Candice couldn't see detail – no mouth, no nose, no eyes. "His head looked like it was hooded, although this figure was all one form and color," she said. "It was very menacing and obviously not a good thing."

Candice's personal life had been in shambles and after spending weeks muddling through fits of sleep, she was wide awake when the entity approached her. "I was really fed up of being so afraid … and I sat up in the bed and I actually took a swing at this thing. I think I said 'fuck you,'" she said. "The instant my fist would have come in contact with it, it instantly vanished. I was shocked, although I'm not sure what I was expecting. I just let my anger and frustration come out."

After the Shadow Thing disappeared, the menacing feeling also left her. "I felt very good after I figured out that I had defeated it that night by swallowing my fear and attacking it," she said. "I have since come to believe that negative entities like this thrive or somehow live off of people's fear."

After her encounter, she gained confidence in herself and her life improved. "My fear level was not as severe and the negative encounters started fading," she said. "I think partly because I stood up to this thing and got angry and confronted it. It's not easy dealing with paranormal things that are impossible to understand, and they can be very traumatic."

All You Need is Anger

Chuck was paralyzed, just frozen in his bed, unable to fight. This is Chuck, a 17-year-old high school state wrestler who also did kickboxing and jujitsu. He was terrified. "It was accompanied with very intense energy vibrating through my body," he said. "It felt like a moderate/high frequency in every cell. Almost as if I was being scanned."

Pinned to the bed, somehow feeling that whatever caused this wanted him to feel overwhelmed, Chuck fought to move any muscle. People in the house were awake. If I could only make a sound, he thought. "I could smell the bacon my grandmother was cooking in the kitchen," he said. "I was fully conscious with my eyes open when I noticed a dark form standing to my right, about eight feet away. It was ominous."

The featureless entity, tall, black, and cloaked, loomed like an omen – then Chuck's anger overwhelmed his fear. "I felt it was responsible for this, and I wanted to destroy it," he said. "I finally was able to move – of all things – my tongue. I wiggled it back and forth and like a key, opening a door ..." the lock over his muscles was gone. "My fist shot out with a right hook and went clean through both sides of the sheet-rock of a wall my bed was against," Chuck said.

It was over. The dark entity was gone.

All You Need is Love

An electric vibration buzzed through the home in the desert near Victorville, California. As Carrie Ann tried to fall asleep, she felt a jolt starting from her feet and moving upwards eventually throughout her whole body. "Being very conscious and afraid of this increasing uncomfortable feeling," she said, "I mentally tried to fight it while thinking of God to rescue me."

And, about a minute later, the feeling left her. "I sat up bug-eyed, thinking this couldn't have been real," she said. But after settling back down 10 minutes later, it happened again. "I tried to fight it," she said. "I released a myriad of emotions the second time from panic, fear, hostility, then helplessness."

The encounter stopped after about 30 seconds, but left Carrie Ann feeling violated. "I was abused, used, and confused," she said. "After I dealt with that, minutes later, I unfortunately experienced it again. This time, after having the 'oh, shit, not again' feelings, I just let it do what it wanted to do."

Once she succumbed to the feeling, it stopped immediately. Carrie Ann thinks she gave the thing what it wanted. "When I was submissive to this intrusive thing, it certainly wasn't as uncomfortable," she said. "I think that was its goal, to make me feel that I was not in control."

A few years later in Northern California, it came to her again, but just once. Two years after that, her sister had the same experience – although Carrie Ann's sister saw her attacker. "She saw a dark Shadow Figure observing her in the corner of her room," she said. "She said it looked like a statue or like the Oscar trophy. It was standing with its arms crossed about 6 1/2 feet tall, broad shoulders and slender lower body – identical to the shape of the ancient Sumerian god statue."

Neither Carrie Ann nor her sister has experienced this entity since, but Carrie Ann said she's ready for it. "I haven't had that feeling in five or six years now, but should it happen again, I will not reward it with fearful emotions," she said. "They do seem to me to be 'psychic vampires,' as some mentioned, sucking on our fear. I am better equipped these days, spiritually strengthened, knowing that love does conquer all. Perhaps this is why they have not returned. Love is the answer."

It Flew Away

Teenager Gloria Dunham was in bed listing to the radio in 2007 when Shadow People invaded her room. "I have trouble sleeping some nights, and was told the radio could help," she said. "I was just turning off the radio when, for some reason, I looked up, and above me were three black, drapey Shadow Figures flying around my bed." She slammed her eyes shut, hoping these figures would go away. Eventually she drifted off to sleep.

"The next night, I was listing to the radio again – to something my parents didn't really approve of," she said. "I had my eyes shut, and I heard a voice, nice and comforting, tell me I was going to get found out."

She pulled her eyes open, certain there was a person in her room. "The voice was so loud and clear, I was sure it was a visible person," she said. "I looked around and suddenly I noticed another Shadow Person flying above my bed. I told it to go away and it stopped and flew away."

The next day, her parents found the music the Shadow Person warned her about. "They were very disappointed in my music choice and took it away," she said. "I was very upset and was crying at night, and then I heard that voice again tell me it was going to be okay and it was. This time I was scared, I yelled at it to go away."

She never heard the voice or saw the Shadow Person again. "You can tell Shadow People to leave you alone," she said. "Maybe they're around you because you're doing something wrong behind someone's back and they're just trying to get you stop."

Protection From the Sgili

Wahde, a Cherokee, said these Shadow People are "sgili," or witches, and the Cherokee have developed ways to protect themselves from the sgili. "There's a lot of protective measures a person can take," Wahde said. "A lot of them have to do with tobacco and prayers. A lot of them have to do with cedar or lightning-struck wood."

Or spit. To the Cherokee, saliva has power. "When [an attack] is going, spit on your hands and grab them. If you know them, shout out their name. If you catch them in that form, you can keep them from going back to their body, and they'll die."

Edged objects also have power over Shadow People. "Take scissors or a knife," he said. "With your saliva on those things, you can stop them. With those things close by, that is usually enough to keep them away."

Leave Me Alone

Margie Kay, psychic and founder of the QUEST paranormal group in Independence, Missouri, said getting rid of a Shadow Person might be as easy as uttering three words. "My daughter, Maria, had an experience with one who followed her from her house to her car one day a few years ago," she said. "It had been in the house a few days, but did not fully materialize until this day. It was very menacing. She looked it straight in the eyes and said 'Leave me alone.'"

The Shadow Person left and did not come back. "I think the key here is, do not show any fear, confront it immediately, and order it to leave," she said, although offered some words of caution. "Maria is a psychic and has had experience working with entities so she knew what she was doing."

Just Ignore Them

Psychic Shane Turnbeaugh from Jefferson City,

Missouri, has dealt with Shadow People and offers his own two words of protection – ignore them.

"I warn my clients not to engage them," Turnbeaugh said. "The cloaked ones, or the ones that appear to be wearing a hooded sweatshirts, seem to feed off of fear, and in many cases these are the ones that in my experience seem to turn that fear into anger and aggression." Although, he believes, all Shadow People have the potential to be aggressive or combative.

"Just like people, they are an energy form and there are some good and some bad," he said. "The best protection is to ignore them. Most of the time they will go away."

If the Shadow Person doesn't leave, then he suggests consulting an expert. "There are other ways to deal with the problem, but that should be left to those of us who are trained psychics/mediums or spiritual advisers," he said. "My advice to my clients who have experiences with these entities is to ignore them and leave them alone. If left alone or ignored, most will simply move on."

There's Nothing We Can Do

The best way to rid your home of Shadow People, said Polly Gear of Mountaineer Ghosts Paranormal Investigators, is for *you* to leave. "To me, this depends on the person seeing it, and it depends on the nature of the Shadow Person, too," she said. "Being a paranormal investigator, I wouldn't run from it at all. Although, a person that is not familiar with seeking paranormal activity would possibly be quite frightened by encountering a Shadow Person in their home."

If a person fears the entity, they can have their home "cleansed" by psychics, or bring in the clergy, although Gear has doubts about these methods of protection. "We have no control over anything paranormal," she said. "So there isn't really much of a choice that anyone can do.

Paranormal activity is going to do what it wants to, when it wants to."

AFTERWORD

I've tried to figure out the Shadow People enigma since I was young – too young to appreciate the finer points of anything, like life, religion, politics, football, philosophy, and *The Dukes of Hazzard*. As a child, Shadow People scared the hell out of me. These entities kept me awake until deep into the dark, dark night while they mingled around my bed, possibly waiting for me to drift awkwardly into sleep. They invaded and terrorized a part of my childhood I've never discussed until now.

One of my most frightening memories came when I called my father late one night because a Shadow Man had walked from my room into the hallway. It wasn't until I realized my dad was walking down that same hallway that the terror struck me – I had called my dad to his doom. Of course, he didn't see any Shadow Man, but I know I did. As an adult I haven't seen Shadow People, and for that I'm thankful. But, as an adult, these entities have plagued my mind even more, as I try to fit them into my grown-up knowledge of the world.

What have we learned about the Shadow Man? We've heard from experts in physics, psychology, Catholicism, Christianity, parapsychology, exorcisms, ghosts, demons, inter-dimensional travel, and extraterrestrials. Many of these experts don't agree on what Shadow People are, but they all agree there is something to the Shadow People phenomenon.

Whatever they are, the many first-person encounters in this book make one point very, very real – Shadow People exist. These entities do walk into our realities, and they do interact with us. Even though the Shadow People that walked through my room as a child didn't seem to take notice of me, they were still interacting with me –

they frightened me.

But this all begs the question: "Now what?" What do we do with this information? We've read about a Cherokee belief that Shadow People are American Indian shamans who have turned to the dark side. Christians and Catholics tell us Shadow Beings are demons. Ghost hunters tell us they're ghosts. Psychologists say they're a natural biochemical reaction or a common sleep state. Psychics say they're all of the above and maybe, just maybe, from another dimension. Physicists can tell you what Shadow People aren't (gravity and Newton's laws of motion don't have a lot of wiggle room). And people who see space ships tell us these entities are from other worlds.

After writing about these encounters, I have to say all the explanations – in some way – are probably right. The common point in all these Shadow People encounters is their appearance. Shadow People are (mostly) human figures, blacker than the night around them. They walk, sometimes awkwardly, and disappear through a wall or in a puff of ether. After that, descriptions of these Shadow People differ, sometimes wildly. The cloaked ones feed off fear, the red-eyed ones bring terror, the Hat Man... well, he wears a hat, and others just seem to be passing through.

Many animals of different breeds that fill the same role in geographically-separated ecosystems are physically similar. The same could be true of Shadow People. But, as psychic Patti Starr of Lexington, Kentucky puts it, "I just don't believe Shadow People can be of just one category or one class. There's so much of it."

But what do these entities want? Our planetary resources? Our life energy? Our souls? Nothing? Their motivation may be as simple as using our plane of existence as the fastest way from Point A to Point B. It may be as complex as alien abduction. Or it may be as horrible as the deep darkness harvesting our souls for nourishment.

I hope that *Darkness Walks* has brought you closer to

an understanding of this profound mystery.

SOURCE AND REFERENCE WEBSITES

- *Allis, Jack*: www.harmonymindbodyspirit.com
- *Auerbach, Loyd*: www.mindreader.com
- *Axe Murder House*: www.villiscaiowa.com
- *Gargiulo, Alexandra*: www.hauntingholzer.com
- *Gear, Polly*: http://www.wvghosts.com/mgrwv/
- *Hebert, Carrie and Murray, Pat*: www.ParanormalResearchersofOhio.com
- *Heron, Patrick*: www.nephilimapocalypse.com
- *Jones, Marie D.*: www.mariedjones.com
- *Kay, Margie*: www.ufokc.4mg.com
- *Lemp Mansion*: www.lempmansion.com
- *Long, Bishop James*: www.universalcatholic.com
- *Lynch, Dr. Michael*: www.michael-lynch.com
- *Marble, Brenda*: www.millersparanormalresearch.com
- *McDonald, Gil Sr.*: cosmostarman.tripod.com/
- *Newlan, Dawn*: Is no longer on the Web.
- *Oester, Dr. Dave*: www.ghostweb.com
- *Offutt, Jason*: from-the-shadows.blogspot.com, shadowpeoplebook.blogspot.com, www.jasonoffutt.com
- *Parsons, D.H.*: www.bliss-parsons.com
- *Rhine Feather, Dr. Sally*: www.rhine.org
- *Starr, Patti*: www.ghosthunter.com
- *Steiger, Brad*: www.bradandsherry.com
- *Straub, Ryan and Tir Firnath Paranormal (e-mail)*: Tir_firnath@hotmail.com
- *Turnbeaugh, Shane*: www.psychicshane.net
- *Walther, Pastor Harry*: www.satansrapture.com
- *Zimmermann, Linda*: www.ghostinvestigator.com

I welcome correspondence on the riddle of the Shadow People. You can leave a comment for me at shadowpeoplebook.blogspot. com, or email me at jasonoffutt@hotmail.com.

Printed in July 2023
by Rotomail Italia S.p.A., Vignate (MI) - Italy